ENGLISH CERAMICS

ENGLISH CERAMICS

By George Savage

PUBLISHERS OF FINE ART BOOKS

New York, New York

First American Edition published in the United States of America in 1961 by
Universe Books, Inc., New York 16, New York.

© 1961 of the original edition:
Office du Livre SA, Fribourg (Switzerland)

Published in 1981 by: The Alpine Fine Arts Collection, Ltd.
527 Madison Avenue, New York, New York 10022
ISBN: 0-933516-15-0
This book was produced in Switzerland

CONTENTS

SINCE THE DAYS OF AUGUSTUS the Strong of Saxony porcelain has been an important facet of European art collecting, and a considerable edifice of knowledge and criticism has been erected round it. Except for Italian maiolica, pottery is a more recent preoccupation, because it was, in the first place, intended for more humble uses, and only in the last hundred years or so has it emerged from the obscurity which previously surrounded it.

Both these things are important in their own way. Apart from being excellent decoration, an absorbing pastime, and even, in these days, a profitable investment, they also throw much light on customs and fashions at the time when they were made. They are, in fact, an essential social document.

It is, perhaps, not often realized that porcelain in particular was held in high esteem during the 18th century. Today it is, for the most part, an article of utility, mass-produced in factories, and formed and decorated by mechanical means, but originally it was so highly regarded that artists of distinction used it as a medium, and Kings and Princes subsidized factories for no better reason than the prestige to be had from so doing. Augustus the Strong, for instance, lavished money on the undertaking at Meissen, and Madame de Pompadour and Louis Quinze assiduously promoted the sale of the products of Sèvres. D'Argenson has recorded that Mme de Pompadour gave an emphatic opinion that not to buy the porcelain of Sèvres was to prove oneself a bad citizen, whilst of Louis Quinze it was said, 'He sells the porcelain himself, and it is not cheap.'

In the 18th century the European attitude almost approached that of the Chinese, who give the ceramic art a very high place in their esteem. Indeed, it is almost the first of all the arts in that country. The intensification of the factory system in the 19th century, allied to the almost universal lowering of standards of taste in the decorative arts, had a particularly vicious impact on pottery and porcelain, and they are only just beginning to emerge again as a significant art form.

The factory system apart, both the Seven Years' War and the neo-classical style had much to do with this debasement of standards. The former was responsible for a progressive loss of the influence previously exerted by a section of society – the aristocracy – which, whatever its defects, preserved a reasonable level of discipline in the arts generally. The bourgeoisie which replaced it had no traditions, and was interested in the arts primarily as a way of displaying a newly acquired wealth. They confused an excess of intricate ornament with good taste. Neo-classicism as a style was particularly unsuited to porcelain as a material. The severe shapes led to an excess of painted ornament, first to be seen in the work of Sèvres, and this tendency was avidly copied elsewhere. The only aspect of neo-classicism which avoided these faults can, in fact, be found in the work of Wedgwood in England.

The origin of the sentimental approach which, unexpectedly perhaps, was combined with neo-classicism can be found in the uuprecedented success of Goethe's novel, 'The Sorrows of Young Werther' (Die Leiden des jungen Werthers), which was based on the story of a fellow student at Leipzig University, who committed suicide because of a hopeless passion for the wife of another man. The receptivity of the rising middle class to mawkish sentiment and superficial emotion caused this to sell an enormous number of copies by 18th century standards. People dressed in the manner of the characters, *Werther* and *Lotte*; scenes from the book were painted on porcelain; and men even committed suicide in imitation of *Werther*. It is difficult to believe that an outbreak of mass hysteria for such reasons could have happened before the Seven Years' War.

England remained largely untouched. If the English character has the defects of its virtues, it also draws a certain amount of strength and stability from its vices. Culture, in the European sense, has always been an exotic plant in English soil, and there has been little patience with strong emotion or its expression.

This is well expressed in both pottery and porcelain, but particularly the former. The things which are peculiarly English also have both feet on the ground, and, more often than not, firmly implanted in the mud. Glancing through the plates which illustrate the section of this book devoted to porcelain, it is easy to pick out the things which have no Continental counterparts. The jug on Plate 116, which depicts men carousing outside an inn, could not have been done on porcelain elsewhere, despite the fleeting fashion for Teniers subjects at Sèvres. It is remarkable, too, how many of the things illustrated in both the pottery and porcelain sections have to do with eating and drinking, particularly the latter. Until the 18th century the Englishman was of the earth, earthy, and most of the finer things which bear comparison with those of the great Continental factories were made by Huguenot emigrés.

Despite the fact that Staffordshire is now one of the largest and most successful concentrations of the industry in the world, the English did little to foster the ceramic art. Even the 18th century factory system was hardly more elaborate and efficient than that in use among the Roman potters of Samian ware nearly two thousand years before, and the first manufacturer consistently to mark pottery was Josiah Wedgwood. Of the porcelain factories, the work of Chelsea and Worcester is marked fairly consistently, that of the others but little until the end of the century.

At a time when almost every Continental country was subsidizing its factories for prestige reasons, England alone expected its manufacturers to survive and operate on a strictly commercial basis. This is, perhaps, to be expected from a country which still spends less on the arts than any other civilized nation, but it is not surprising that only one porcelain factory which existed during the 18th century now survives.

What, then, is the fascination which both English pottery and porcelain have always exercised over the collector? Some of it is undoubtedly due to the fact that it has an artistry and an individuality of its own. It is evocative of the men who made it. It lacks, too, the slickness – the professional touch – of the Continental potter, and the technical difficulties of manufacture are usually quite apparent. We can, therefore, enter vicariously into the perplexities and troubles of those who made it. Lastly, it is a challenge to the intellect. Unlike Continental factories there are no archives of consequence on which to base its history. This must be put together from fragmentary records – letters, advertisements, contemporary mention in diaries and biographies – and from the physical nature of the objects themselves. It forms, for this reason, a series of problems which, for the most part, can only be partially resolved, and about which there is always something to be learned.

Therefore the pages which follow must, of necessity, be principally concerned with biographical material and contemporary records. These go to make up a story of absorbing interest, in which the various parts are seen to be interdependent. The text is indispensable to an understanding of the illustrations, which have been selected both as outstanding examples of their kind, and as links in the evidential chain.

8

FIRST PART: POTTERY

MEDIEVAL AND TIN-ENAMELED WARES

WHILST the pottery and porcelain of England has, at some periods, depended for inspiration on that of the Continent, there are many original features which are the direct result of its insular position.

The earliest specimens of English pottery belong to a period between about 2500 and 1900 B.C. – usually designated the Neolithic, or New Stone Age. Nomadic hunters do not make pots, and pottery invariably marks the transition between hunting and food collecting and a settled, agricultural, way of life. It is a curious sidelight on the pottery of primitive peoples everywhere that pots which are made by hand modeling and coiling are the work of the women of the tribe, and men did not become potters until the introduction of the wheel.

In England the potter's wheel came into use about 450 B.C., and the Roman invasion brought with it more sophisticated techniques. Raids and incursions by Continental peoples who followed the departure of the Roman legions plunged the country into internecine strife, and for a long period it was divided into virtually autonomous kingdoms, fighting for bare survival against marauding Vikings. When unity was at last achieved, the King sat uneasily on his throne, and his *fiat* ran no further than his armies could march.

Vessels for the service of food on the rude tables of the poor were made from wood, and those to be found in the strongholds of the powerful were rarely better. Few specimens of pottery of this period have survived, and most of them are hardly an improvement on those of the Iron Age.

English pottery does not begin to develop once more until after the invasion of William of Normandy in 1066, when the country once more began to enjoy settled conditions. Centuries still had to pass before production could be concentrated in such centers as Staffordshire – the focal point of the modern industry.

English medieval pottery was made locally for local needs. The workshops were small, with, perhaps, one or two wheels. Communications, too, were bad, roads being impassable during the frequent periods of wet weather, and even as late as the 18th century it was often easier, during the winter, to travel between London and the South Coast by sea.

Written records are extremely scanty, and it is impossible to identify potters and places of manufacture until about the middle of the 16th century.

These wares are made from clays which burned in the kiln to a color varying between buff and dark red, or less often, to a grayish-black. This is due to the presence of small quantities of iron oxide as an impurity, and the effect is commonly to be seen in pottery throughout the world. The body varied in hardness, but it is always a porous earthenware. The earlier specimens to be recovered are unglazed, although it is possible that glazes were used during Saxon times. The practice of glazing did not become widespread until after the Norman Conquest, and it was probably brought from France, where a lead glaze was in use before the 13th century. This, however, provided the extent of such borrowings. English medieval pottery is quite separate and distinct from contemporary French wares in form and proportion.

The color of the glazes used varies between yellow and brown for the most part, but an excellent green was attained by mixing copper filings with the glaze material, and a rich brown of purplish hue came from the application of the glaze over a slip (that is, clay which had been diluted to the consistency of cream) to which manganese had been added.

Nearly all surviving specimens of medieval pottery are jugs and vessels for containing liquids, but some excellent tilework was done, principally for the decoration of walls and pavements in churches. Inlaying in white slip can be seen on tiles from Chertsey Abbey made during the latter part of the 13th century.

Survivals of wares made during the 16th century are more frequent, and more diverse. 'Cistercian' ware is so-called because much of it has been discovered in the ruins of Cistercian Abbeys in Yorkshire. The body is hard, and covered with an excellent dark brown glaze with a metallic appearance (Plate 9). A much greater degree of precision in the formation and finish is to be noticed. It is said that after the Dissolution of the Monasteries in 1540 this ware was no longer made, but the statement is erroneous.

Whilst the potters of England were still in the Bronze Age, the Assyrians were making decorative courses of brick covered with a glaze made white and opaque with tin oxide. This glaze fell into disuse, but the secret was rediscovered by Middle Eastern potters some time before the 9th century A.D. The expansion of Islam took it to Moorish Spain, whence it spread to Italy during the early part of the 15th century. Here it was used for the important class of Renaissance pottery known as *maiolica*. The art of tin enameling soon spread to France, Germany, and Holland, and, from the latter country, it crossed the sea to England.

The most important difference between the tin-enamel glazes and those in use hitherto is that the former provided a white surface on which it was possible to paint in a number of colors, the most usual being cobalt blue. The other colors – known as high-temperature pigments because they were fired at the same temperature as the glaze – include green from copper, purple from manganese, yellow from antimony, and an orange red from iron.

This new ware, which reached England in the middle of the 16th century, was called 'gallyware,' and Stow's *Survey of London*, published in 1598, mentions Jacob Jansson and Jasper Andries, Dutch potters, as being at work in London in 1570. It is probable that Andries was a kinsman of a potter from Castel Durante in Italy – one Guido da Savino, who called himself Andries. This man settled in Antwerp in 1512.

The earliest specimens of English tin enamel, however, were not made by Jansson and Andries. These have a general resemblance to the form of the Rhineland stoneware jugs from Cologne which were popular in England at the time, but the mottled salt glaze (known as 'tigerware') was replaced by a tin glaze splashed with blue and purple or blue and yellow, or sometimes with a monochrome blue or turquoise glaze only. Many of these were mounted in pewter or silver, and the earliest, in the British Museum, has a silver mount with the datemark for 1549. One such jug was formerly in the Church of West Malling in Kent, and they have been given the generic name of 'Malling' jugs. Where they were made is not clear, but London is most likely. These jugs range in date from 1549 to the early years of the 17th century, but they can only be dated from any hallmark appearing on the mount.

A few examples of tin-enameled ware, one or two of which distantly recall Italian *maiolica*, have survived from the end of the 16th century, and some may well be the work of Jansson and Andries. The first dated example of this kind is shown on Plate 2, and was made in the year 1600. By this time potters were established on the South Bank of the Thames at Southwark, and they later started work at Lambeth and Bermondsey also. A feature of the dated dish illustrated is an outer border of blue dashes, and this later becomes a familiar *motif* on a long series of dishes decorated with fruit and foliage in the Italian manner, with Biblical subjects (Plate 3), Kings of England, ships, and so forth. These were made over a considerable period of time, surviving into the 18th century, and they are usually called 'blue dash' chargers.

In 1602 the Portuguese carrack, the *San Jago*, was captured by the Dutch, and brought as a prize to Middelburg. This contained much Chinese porcelain made during the reign of the Ming Emperor, Wan Li. In 1604 vast quantities of porcelain arrived in Holland, and this, too, had been captured from the Portuguese. James I of England bought some of the cargo, and the fashion for Chinese porcelain in Northern Europe had been born.

Soon, these Chinese wares were being copied in Holland, painted in blue on a tin glaze and called 'Hollandsche porselein,' and English potters were hardly behind their Dutch rivals. We find mugs and small jugs painted in blue with copies of such Wan Li *motifs* as birds amid rock and foliate patterns. These bear dates from 1628 onwards. Sometimes the name of the owner, or an inspiring aphorism was added (Plate 13).

At this time we can see a curious mixture of styles and patterns taken from China, and from Italy. A few specimens are based on the work of Bernard Palissy and his followers in France – a dish with a molded design taken from Titian's *La Fécondité*, for instance. Others imitate the *bleu Persan* of Nevers, and are either mottled in white on a blue ground, or are painted in white with simple patterns.

Towards mid-century wine bottles became a popular article of manufacture in London. Many are dated, and they range from 1639 to about 1670. Usually they have the name of the wine thereon – 'Sack' (sherry), 'Rhenish' (the white wine of the Rhineland), or 'Whit' (probably white Bordeaux). Opinion is divided on whether these bottles contained samples, or whether they were for table use. It is probable that the latter is the case, and the date is that on which they were bottled in London from the cask. To my knowledge, only one polychrome example exists.

Other vessels connected with the service of wine and similar potable liquors include the puzzle jug which has a perforated neck, the fuddling cup (a series of interlaced cups, the purpose of which was to 'fuddle' the drinker), and the posset pot (Plate 19) which held a mixture of hot spiced milk and ale. Punch bowls were made from about 1680, and the 'Monteith,' a bowl with a scalloped rim to hold wine glasses by the foot, can be seen occasionally, although it is more familiar in silver.

Apothecary wares include various drug jars. The *albarello* (Plate 12) is ultimately derived from the Middle East, and has a long history as an apothecary jar. A spouted globular version on a high foot (for wet drugs) is perhaps the more frequent survival. These usually bear the name of the drug, and often initials and a date. Pill slabs, for rolling pills, bear the Arms of the Apothecaries' Company (Plate 18). The popular remedy for most ills, bloodletting, was responsible for the manufacture of bleeding bowls, hardly distinguishable from porringers, except that they have one handle instead of two.

By the middle of the 17th century the potters of the town of Delft, in Holland, were taking over the disused breweries of that City, and the industry was expanding rapidly. Dutch potters came to England, and their native styles affected the decoration of tin-enameled wares in England. The Dutch wares soon became known as delft, and the name was applied to English wares of the same kind. In 1671 there is record of a patent granted to John Ariens van Hamme, resident in London, whilst other potters arrived in the train of William, Prince of Orange, when he succeeded to the throne of England. Among the things which we assume to have been done by them are a set of six plates, each of which bears a separate line of doggerel:

> 'What is a Merry Man
> Let him doe what hee kan
> To entertain his gests
> With wine and merry jests
> But if his wife do frowne
> All merriment goes downe'

A full, matching, set is a great rarity.

Other things made by these Dutch potters working in London resemble the delft of Holland so closely that confusion between Dutch and English wares is common.

During the 18th century copies of Chinese wares are particularly frequent, and a mixture of European subjects and Chinese decorative *motifs* is not infrequent. As the century progressed, the influence of the French *rococo* style is to be seen. This affected English decorative art somewhat later than its appearance on the Continent, and it is well seen in the work of the Huguenot silversmith, Paul Lamerie.

The neo-classical style – the revival of Greek and Roman styles resulting from the discovery of the sites of Herculaneum and Pompeii – was not particularly used by the makers of delft. It did not translate well into tin-enameled pottery, and the popularity of the style played a part in the decline of manufacture, although the principal cause was undoubtedly the rise of Wedgwood's creamware, later discussed.

Although the principal factories were situated at Lambeth and Southwark in London, a flourishing manufacture existed also in Bristol, where a beginning was made about 1650. Some of the 'blue dash' chargers already mentioned were made here, but the greater part of the production was of blue painted ware with fantastic Chinese scenes, most of which could accurately be termed *chinoiseries*. The influence of Dutch potters is often strong in the early period, and painting in white on a bluish ground (Plate 21) is a derivation from Italian *maiolica* which was almost a Bristol specialty.

A factory at Wincanton, in Somerset, made much use of manganese purple in its decoration, whilst Liverpool used ships as a *motif* freely. Much transfer-printed ware was also made at Liverpool. This process was claimed as an independent invention by Sadler & Green of that city (see page 269). Apart from transfer printing, almost all the wares described were painted on the raw glaze before firing. This was a difficult operation, the glaze in this state absorbing color like ink on blotting paper. Erasures were impossible. Slight use was made of enamel colors, that is, those painted on the glaze after firing and fixed in a low-temperature muffle kiln in the manner of porcelain. Existing specimens seem, mostly, to have been made in Liverpool, and the enamels are often confined to the addition of red and yellow to the high-temperature colors already used (Plate 4). Transfer printing on delft is, of course, a kind of enamel decoration, since it is done on the glaze.

The manufacture of delft ceased in England at the end of the 18th century.

SLIP WARE

LIP IS clay mixed to the consistency of cream, and it is used for a variety of purposes. Clay which is poor in color, but otherwise satisfactory, may be given a surface wash of slip of a more attractive color – white over a red body, for instance. Decoration may subsequently be incised through the slip to the body underneath, the differently colored clays forming an effective pattern (*sgraffito* ware). Slip may be painted on with a brush, as in the case of the medieval jug illustrated on Plate 6, and it may be dotted and trailed in the same way as a confectioner uses icing-sugar to decorate a cake (Plate 25). All these ways of using slip need a glaze to protect it from wear and tear.

These techniques can all be seen on English pottery of one kind or another, but only the trailed slip variety can be classified into a coherent group of ware. Most such pottery is peasant ware, made for local markets, and the earliest came from the area of Wrotham, in Kent, a village between Sevenoaks and Maidstone. Much work was done here by George Richardson and Nicholas Hubble about the middle of the 17th century, and dated examples range from about 1612 (Plate 24). Wrotham was probably making a lead-glazed ware in the 16th century, and it was still doing so in the early part of the 18th.

Most existing specimens are tygs, a kind of communal drinking cup with three double-looped handles. Many are dated, and bear initials stamped on to clay pads of a light color applied to the red clay body before glazing. The slip ornament was added in dots, and in geometric patterns, the handles being lined in the same way. Apart from the tygs, posset pots and jugs are also to be seen. Candlesticks seem peculiar to Wrotham, and dishes are extremely rare.

The manufacture of slipware was established in London by 1630, and it appears to have been, for much of the time, in the hands of Puritans. In the words of Sir Steuart Wilson, the Puritans regarded birth as the entry to sin, marriage as a way of avoiding one aspect of it, and death as a welcome relief, whereby they could sin no more, and many of the London dishes bear pious exhortations such as 'Fast and Pray,' 'Feare God,' and 'Remember thy End,' in trailed slip. This is a notable variation on the work of the Wrotham sinners, who were principally engaged in making drinking cups. Specimens of London manufacture are usually referred to as 'Metropolitan.'

Soon after the middle of the 17th century manufacture seems to have been concentrated in Staffordshire. Few Metropolitan specimens can be awarded a date much later than that of the accession of Charles II, and no doubt the colorful delft pottery appealed to the prevailing spirit of the times rather more than the grim reminders of sin and mortality which marked the Commonwealth period.

The principal maker of trailed slip ware in Staffordshire appears to have been Thomas Toft, and about thirty dishes bearing his name are known. An example in the Chester Museum is dated 1672.

These dishes bear such designs as the Royal Arms, the Lion and the Unicorn (from the English Royal Arms), an amusing Mermaid, the Pelican in her Piety (Plate 5), Charles II hiding in the Boscobel oak (represented by his head protruding through the foliage), some crude portraits of such members of the Royal Family as the Duke of York and Catherine of Braganza, and the like. The ledge usually has a decoration of trellised or other geometric ornament, with a panel reserved at the bottom for the name of the potter. Apart from dishes, the name of Toft occurs on certain rare examples of hollow ware, notably a tyg in York Museum. Cradles (Plate 27) were made as marriage gifts, and were probably fertility symbols.

Thomas Toft was a member of a family which appears to have come from Leek on the Staffordshire border, and James, Charles, and Ralph Toft are also recorded, a dish by Ralph in the British Museum being dated 1676. The work of Toft provided inspiration for other makers of slip ware, and, of these, perhaps the best are signed by Ralph Simpson. Many other names have been recorded, some from existing specimens, and others on slender evidence. The fact that many such dishes are signed and some are dated makes it possible that they had a commemorative purpose which now escapes us.

The technique, in most cases, is similar. The designs were executed in white, brown, and red slip over a reddish body, the whole being covered with a yellowish glaze which modifies the color of the slips. Designs are crude, but executed in an amusing and vigorous style.

Trailed slip decoration continued to be used on 'peasant' wares throughout the 18th century in Staffordshire, at Tickenhall in Derbyshire, and elsewhere. Isolated specimens from such minor centers of manufacture as Yorkshire and Sussex bear dates almost to the end of the century, the latest, apparently, being 1797 on a Yorkshire bottle in a private collection.

Sgraffito wares were made at Wrotham at the end of the 17th century, and they occur from Staffordshire during the 17th and 18th centuries. The latter are sometimes (erroneously) associated with the name of Ralph Shaw. *Sgraffito* work of good quality was also done towards the end of the 18th century in the West of England.

'Marbled' wares, in which a contrasting slip was 'combed' or 'feathered' to produce an effect similar to the marbled end papers of some 18th century books, came from Staffordshire (Plate 28). The process was sometimes combined with trailed slip decoration.

Wares ornamented with incised or stamped patterns inlaid with slip of contrasting color, a technique recalling certain medieval tiles, were made in Sussex from the latter part of the 18th century onwards.

1. JUG. MEDIEVAL POTTERY. 14TH CENTURY

26 cm. The London Museum, Kensington Palace

Found at Whitehall, in the City of Westminster, this jug has a red body covered with a slightly mottled green glaze derived from copper oxide. The handle is indented with a thumbprint at the grip, and the base has four alternating sets of four and three thumbprints, equally spaced. This was done to level the base, and the practice was fairly common. This jug, typical of the best medieval wares, is monumental in form, and its simplicity makes it extremely attractive.

2. PLATE. TIN-ENAMELED WARE. LONDON. 1600

25.75 cm. The London Museum, Kensington Palace

The inscription on this dish makes it the earliest known example of tin-enameled ware painted in high-temperature colors which can be accurately dated. The body is buff, and covered with a grayish tin enamel. The border of grotesque heads suggests the indirect influence of Italian *maiolica* from Deruta. The buildings in the central medallion are probably a view of contemporary London.

3. DISH. TIN-ENAMELED WARE. C. 1675

40.5 cm. The Victoria and Albert Museum (Schreiber Collection), London

This charger (a name sometimes given to large flat dishes) belongs to the 'blue dash' group – so-called from the border pattern. The earliest known use of these blue dashes may be seen on the dish illustrated on Plate 2. These dishes first appeared in their later form about 1660, and were made until the first decades of the 18th century. Specimens are claimed for both Bristol and London, but there is no certainty in the matter. The subject is the Fall of Man, drawn in a primitive and amusing style. The colors are simple high-temperature *faïence* pigments.

4. PLATE. TIN-ENAMELED WARE. LIVERPOOL. C. 1760

34 cm. The Victoria and Albert Museum, London

The palette of this plate has become associated with a Liverpool potter, Thomas Fazackerly. The surface is bluish in tone, and the blue, sage-green, and manganese colors are high-temperature pigments. The red and yellow are both enamels used *over* the tin enamel, and fired later in the muffle kiln.

2

4

5. DISH. SLIP WARE. STAFFORDSHIRE. C. 1685

43 cm. The Syndics of the Fitzwilliam Museum, Cambridge

This dish represents the subject known as the 'Pelican in her Piety.' It is not unusual in all kinds of decorative art, and shows a pelican feeding her young with her own flesh and blood. Alfred de Musset refers to this curious concept (*La Nuit de Mai*), and it was widely believed at the time this dish was made. For instance, *Love for Love* by Congreve (produced in 1695) has this line:

'What, wouldst thou have me turn pelican, and feed thee from my own vitals.'

The dish is typical of the finest Staffordshire slip ware of the period, and shows exceptional qualities of design. After Thomas Toft (page 15), Ralph Simpson is the best-known maker of this kind of ware.

---

6. JUG. MEDIEVAL POTTERY. 13TH CENTURY

30 cm. The Hastings Museum and Art Gallery, Hastings, Sussex

This jug, excavated at Rye in Sussex, is typically medieval in form. It is made from a red-burning clay covered with a yellowish glaze, and the simple painted decoration, admirably adapted to the form, is in cream-white slip. The strap handle is grooved.

---

7. JUG. MEDIEVAL WARE. 14TH CENTURY

35.5 cm. The London Museum, Kensington Palace

This jug is decorated with chevrons of cream slip, with alternating bands of cream and brown at the neck, and dotted slip ornament between the chevrons. The whole is covered with a yellow glaze. These stripes and dots in slip represent the earliest English use of the technique later to be taken up at Wrotham (Plate 24) and Staffordshire (Plate 25). A medieval example of painting with slip is shown on Plate 6.

---

8. NECK OF A PITCHER. MEDIEVAL POTTERY. 14TH CENTURY

21 cm. The London Museum, Kensington Palace

This example, strongly modeled, is the neck of a large pitcher. The remainder has been lost. It is covered with an uneven green glaze, slightly iridescent as the result of burial, over a buff body. The features are pinched between finger and thumb, the hands and mouth have been knife-cut, and the eyes appear to have been made with some kind of circular stamp. This is probably a distant ancestor of the Toby jug illustrated on Plate 63.

7

9

13

15 16

OPIFERQUE PER ORBEM DICOR

18

21

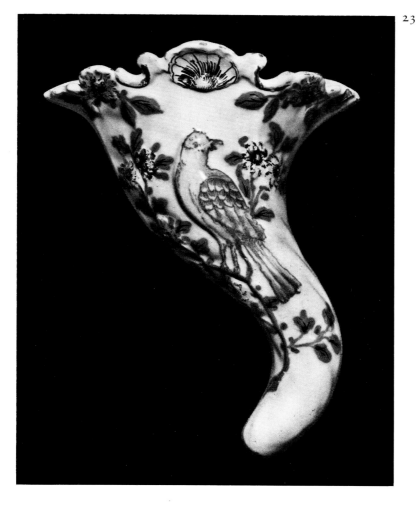

24

26

27

28

29

9. TANKARD. CISTERCIAN WARE. 16TH CENTURY

27 cm. The London Museum, Kensington Palace

A tankard of tall tapering form with a high handle. It is covered with a dark brown glaze with a silvery iridescence over a dark red body. It is decorated with an incised chevron motif, and with concentric circles at top and bottom. The formal relationship between the shape and the position of the handle is interesting. Wares of this kind are attributed to the Cistercian monks, and have been excavated on the sites of former monasteries.

10. WATERING POT. PERHAPS SUSSEX. 16TH CENTURY

28 cm. The Hastings Museum and Art Gallery, Hastings, Sussex

The body is red in color, and is covered with a light brownish-yellow glaze. The handle shows the impress of the potter's fingers where it is joined to the body. These watering pots are a not unusual survival, but it is rare to find one in such good condition.

11. CANDLE SCONCE. C. 1600

Height 44 cm. The Brighton Art Gallery and Museum (Willett Collection), Brighton, Sussex

This sconce, pierced for attachment to the wall, has a yellow glaze with touches of copper green around the candleholders. The Royal Arms are molded above the Tudor Rose. It was formerly at Hampton Court Palace.

12. ALBARELLO. TIN-ENAMELED WARE. END 16TH CENTURY

23 cm. The London Museum, Kensington Palace

This specimen, excavated in London, is painted in alternate manganese and light blue on a pinkish tin-enamel glaze. Although some drug jars of this kind were probably made in Holland, an attribution to London for many of them is reasonable, and they are no doubt similar to the wares made by Andries and Jansson (page 10). The *albarello* was much used by apothecaries. Its origin is in Persia, and it can be seen both in Italian *maiolica* and Hispano-Moresque ware. The specimen shown is slightly waisted, but the incurves of the sides were often much more pronounced with the object of making it easy to remove from a shelf of similar jars. Gaily colored apothecary jars were fashionable in Italy, and such wares generally form a distinct and interesting group.

13. MUG. TIN-ENAMELED WARE. LONDON. 1630

15.5 cm. The London Museum, Kensington Palace

This mug has a tin-enamel glaze over a buff body. The decoration is in blue, and the bands of birds, rocks, flowers, and the like are taken from Chinese motifs used on porcelain made during the reign of the Emperor Wan Li (1573–1619) which was freely exported to European markets. It is an example of a rare early group of wares, and is inscribed:

James and Elizabeth Greene Anno 1630.
The gift is small – goodwill is all.

---

14. DISH. TIN-ENAMELED WARE. LONDON. 1649

39 cm. The Brighton Museum and Art Gallery (Willett Collection), Brighton, Sussex

This gadrooned dish bears the Arms of the Parish Clerks of London (here spelled phonetically – The Clarkes) surrounded by shipping scenes and buildings in blue. The gadrooned form appears both in French and German *faïence*. The decoration is unusually fine for the period, and there is a touch of yellow at the base of the scrollwork surrounding the Arms. These slight passages of color in addition to the predominant blue can be seen again in Plate 18.

---

15. PUTTO. TIN-ENAMELED WARE. LONDON. C. 1650

26 cm. The British Museum, London

This amusing winged *putto* seems to be holding his floral wreath against a high wind. The features, drapery, and pedestal are colored a rich blue. Such figures in tin-enameled ware are extremely rare.

---

16. JUG. TIN-ENAMELED WARE. LAMBETH. 1672

17 cm. The Brighton Art Gallery and Museum (Willett Collection), Brighton, Sussex

This amusing jug, modeled in the form of a seated cat, is decorated with a tin-enamel glaze over a buff body, and is painted in blue, lined to imitate fur. The intitials, RSI, are accompanied by the date, 1672. Similar cats were made in Staffordshire during the first half of the 18th century in agate ware, but Lambeth cats, such as this, are extremely rare. Lady Charlotte Schreiber, recording the purchase of a similar specimen in her journals (November, 1884) remarks:

'My cat belonged, as I suspected, to Mr. Willett – I can only suppose he parts with it because he has two older and better specimens, viz. 1672 and 1674.'

Lady Charlotte's purchase is now in the Schreiber Collection at the Victoria and Albert Museum.

---

17. DISH. TIN-ENAMELED WARE. C. 1680

25 cm. The Victoria and Albert Museum, London

A 'blue dash' charger vigorously decorated with tulips in yellow, green, manganese, and blue – blue being used both for the dashes, and for the outlines of the flowers and leaves. Tulips were a popular motif in the decorative art of the time. See also the remarks accompanying Plate 3.

18. PILL-ROLLING SLAB. TIN-ENAMELED WARE
LONDON. C. 1685

28 × 24 cm. The London Museum, Kensington Palace

This pill-rolling slab of heraldic shield form is decorated in blue with scrolling acanthus leaves, and the Arms of the Apothecaries' Company between two unicorn supporters. The dragon (center) is painted in green. Another example illustrated by Professor F. H. Garner (*English Delftware*) also bears the Arms of the City of London.

---

19. POSSET POT. TIN-ENAMELED WARE. LONDON. C. 1690

18 cm. The Victoria and Albert Museum, London

This spouted pot was made for posset, a mixture of hot spiced ale and milk. The decoration is in blue, and is a later version of the patterns derived from Chinese porcelain to be seen on the mug shown on Plate 13. This is an obvious silver pattern, and was probably derived in the first place from certain very rare spouted tankards of the mid-17th century.

---

20. SAUCEBOAT. TIN-ENAMELED WARE. LAMBETH. C. 1760

Length 20 cm. The Victoria and Albert Museum (Mellor Bequest), London

All tin-enameled pottery was made in a soft earthenware body. Apart from plates, therefore, which were made in enormous quantities, it is rare to find service ware in reasonably good condition. A service containing many plates, for example, would only have one or two sauceboats, and their scarcity is understandable. Most tin-enameled ware was discarded when broken before such things became collectors' items. This sauceboat is of a silver pattern, and is decorated in blue with attractive shipping scenes within *rococo* scroll borders.

---

21. PLATE. TIN-ENAMELED WARE. BRISTOL. C. 1760

22.5 cm. The Victoria and Albert Museum (Schreiber Collection), London

This plate, which has a scalloped rim, is covered with a grayish-blue tin enamel, and the ledge is decorated with floral and foliate motifs in opaque white enamel – the *bianco sopra bianco* technique borrowed from Italian *maiolica*. This style in decoration is relatively common at Bristol, and can also be seen occasionally from Liverpool. The center of the plate is painted with an amusing combination of European and Chinese *motifs* in blue.

---

22. TEAPOT. TIN-ENAMELED WARE. LIVERPOOL. C. 1765

13 cm. The Victoria and Albert Museum (Gift: Sir Wm. Lawrence, Bart.), London

All tea ware in tin-enameled pottery is very scarce. The body is soft earthenware, and the glaze extremely liable to damage. Moreover, teapots rarely withstood boiling water without cracking, and the crack to be observed in the body of this specimen may have been caused in this way. Early porcelain teapots suffered from the same defect, and Worcester made a particular point of the freedom of their porcelain from this shortcoming. The only ware, apart from Worcester, to withstand boiling water successfully was salt-glazed stoneware. This teapot is decorated in a combination of colors – manganese outlines, blue and sage green in the high-temperature range, and touches of red and yellow enamels typical of some of the work of Liverpool (see also Plate 4).

---

23. WALL POCKET. TIN-ENAMELED WARE. LIVERPOOL. C. 1765

21.5 cm. The Victoria and Albert Museum (Mellor Bequest), London

A molded cornucopia, or wall pocket, decorated in blue and green high-temperature *faïence* colors, with touches of red and yellow enamel. Similar things were made at Worcester in porcelain, and in salt-glazed stoneware, but tin-enameled specimens are extremely rare. Another example of the use of the red and yellow enamel on Liverpool tin-enameled ware may be seen on Plate 4.

---

24. TYG. SLIP WARE. WROTHAM, KENT. 1649

16 cm. The Victoria and Albert Museum (Wallace Elliot Bequest), London

This is typical of early slip ware from Wrotham. The ground is dark brown over a red body, the decoration being carried out, for the most part, in a lighter colored clay. The medallion and the date are in relief on light colored clay tablets which were applied. On the reverse are the initials, IL and CWS. The former is thought to refer to John Livermore. Two of the handles are here shown.

---

25. DISH. SLIP WARE. STAFFORDSHIRE. C. 1685

43 cm. The Syndics of the Fitzwilliam Museum, Cambridge

This large portrait dish by Ralph Simpson of Burslem is decorated with light brown, dark brown, and cream slip. Unlikely as it may seem, the figure appears to be intended as a portrait of Charles II. A somewhat similar dish by Thomas Toft bears the monogram CR.

---

26. DISH. SLIP WARE. STAFFORDSHIRE. C. 1690

43 cm. The Brighton Art Gallery and Museum (Willett Collection), Brighton, Sussex

This dish has a red body, yellow background, light brown areas, and details in dark brown. It bears the Royal Arms, and is signed by William Tallor, probably the William Taylor whose work is also represented in the Glaisher Collection (Fitzwilliam Museum) and the British Museum. In the former collection, the name is spelled 'Talor.'

27. CRADLE. SLIP WARE. STAFFORDSHIRE. C. 1690

Length 28 cm. Height 16.5 cm.
The Victoria and Albert Museum (Gift: C. H. Campbell, Esq.), London

The purpose of these cradles is a little obscure, but they were probably given to newly married couples to induce fertility. Alternatively, they may have been used as christening gifts, but this is less likely. Sympathetic magic was far from unknown in England during the 17th century. This example has a light buff body covered with cream slip, with details in dark brown slip. On the reverse are the letters INE:HENS.

28. MUG. SLIP WARE. STAFFORDSHIRE. C. 1710

11 cm. The Victoria and Albert Museum, London

This mug is decorated with yellow and brown slip over a red body by the technique known as 'feathering.' Generally, this is slightly later than the use of trailed slip.

29. POSSET POT. SLIP WARE. STAFFORDSHIRE. 1710

19 cm. The Victoria and Albert Museum, London

This specimen is decorated with yellow and dark brown slip. It has three handles, two of which are shown, and three looped clay strips applied. The inscription, in full, is as follows:

TOMAS DAKIN MADE TIS CUP FOR MARY
SCULL THARP OR FOR HER FREND AD
1710

The following is probably the correct reading:

Thomas Dakin made this cup for Mary / Scullthorp(e) or for her friend AD / 1710. Posset pots in slip ware are exceedingly rare, and this is an exceptionally fine example.

47

ENGLISH STONEWARE

THE STONEWARES of the Rhineland – of Cologne, Raeren, Siegburg, and Westerwald – were especially popular in England, and a large and thriving export trade grew up. The white stoneware tankards (*Schnellen*) of Siegburg have been found in excavations in London, but by far the most popular was a big-bellied stoneware ale bottle, usually with an applied mask on the neck. This mask was thought to be a caricature of the hated Cardinal Bellarmino, and the vessel became known as a 'bellarmine.' The German name for these jugs was '*Bartmannkrug*,' and they were also known in England as 'greybeards.' The principal center for manufacture was Cologne, and such things were often called 'Cologne-ware' in England. Those with a mottled brown glaze, by far the most frequent, were called 'tigerware,' and this glaze effect was imitated in tin enamel on some of the 'Malling' jugs already discussed.

During the early part of the 17th century there are several references to patents for making an imitation of this German stoneware, but it seems unlikely that anything of the kind was made before the advent of John Dwight of Fulham, in London, who took out a patent for the 'mistery and invention of making transparent earthenware, commonly knowne by the names of porcelaine or china, and of stoneware vulgarly called Cologne ware' in 1671.

Stoneware of any kind had not previously been manufactured in Europe, except in Germany. It is a partially vitrified substance, the clay being mixed with sand and other fusible materials, and it is fired at a much higher temperature than earthenware. Although lead glazes were sometimes used on stoneware bodies, most such wares were glazed with salt. A shovelful of salt was thrown into the kiln when it had reached maximum temperature, and the heat split the salt into its component sodium and chlorine. The sodium combined with the silica in the body to form a 'smear' glaze of sodium silicate which appears to be slightly pitted, like the skin of an orange. The chlorine passed out of the kiln chimney. Occasionally, a little red lead was mixed with the salt, and the glaze is then thicker and more glossy in appearance. Stoneware is an important step towards the manufacture of porcelain, because both require a much greater degree of controlled heat than the softer earthenware. In particular the degree of heat required to fire a successful porcelain body is very high, and much was learned about the design of high-temperature kilns from this earlier work with stoneware.

The Fulham factory belonging to Dwight imitated German wares (Plate 35), but it also made other kinds of stoneware. No porcelain can be attributed to it, but some thinly-potted vessels in a grayish-white body are also slightly translucent in places, and translucency in Europe was regarded as the principal test for the porcellaneous nature of a ware. Dwight also made a superb series of figures, here represented by Plates 36 and 37, thought to have been modeled by the sculptor and wood carver, Grinling Gibbons (1648–1721).

Dwight took action in 1693 against several persons for infringement of his patent. Among them were two brothers, John Philip and David Elers, later makers of red stoneware at Bradwell Wood in Staffordshire, and James Morley, a stoneware potter of Nottingham. In 1869, Lady Charlotte Schreiber, the noted collector of English pottery and porcelain, whose collections are now in the Victoria and Albert Museum in London, discovered Dwight's notebooks at Fulham. The entries cover a period of ten years, and include a note of some of the formulae used at the factory, they mention both 'a fine white porcellane clay to be burned with salt' and 'a deep red porcellane or china clay.' These notebooks have since been lost, but a manuscript copy is in the British Museum.

The mention of the deep red clay is particularly important. Tea, as a beverage, arrived in England soon after the middle of the 17th century. It was first brought to Europe by the Dutch in 1645. The shippers sent with it supplies of certain spouted pots in an unglazed stoneware, usually dark brown in color, which were made at Yi-Hsing, in the Chinese Province of Kiangsu. These were thought to make extremely good tea, as, indeed, they do. Since few beverages before this date needed infusion, the making of tea presented some problems. In some instances, at least, tea was infused in large quantities and stored in casks, being drawn off and reheated as required. The popularity of Yi-Hsing pots, therefore, is understandable, and the demand was such that they were speedily copied in Europe, particularly by Arij de Milde in Holland during the 17th century, and by E. W. von Tschirnhaus and J. F. Böttger at Meissen during the first decades of the 18th.

The 'red porcellane' of Dwight was yet another copy of these Yi-Hsing wares, but it is difficult almost to the point of impossibility to identify specimens made at Fulham with certainty.

One more Fulham product (perhaps the commonest survival) needs to be noticed. This takes the form of a series of mugs made in a gray stoneware body, the upper part glazed brown. They are ornamented with applied reliefs, a typical example, dated 1729, being of a pack of hounds and a hare, with the inscription:

> 'On Banse downs a hair we found
> That led us all a Smoaking round.'

Such things were made for taverns and do not appear until after Dwight's death in 1703. A fine specimen of remarkably large size is shown on Plate 38.

Imitations of Fulham stoneware were probably made in Staffordshire during the last years of the 17th century, and a flourishing manufacture was established at Nottingham by James Morley before 1693. Morley had been a party to the action for infringement brought by Dwight in that year. The dark brown glaze has a peculiar metallic appearance which is to be seen on most wares of the kind from Nottingham. Inscriptions scratched into the clay are fairly common, and many specimens are dated, the latest recorded being, apparently, 1774. From Nottingham came jugs with a detachable head in the form of a bear, somewhat similar to the example shown on Plate 57. These were probably related to the German *Eulenkrüge* (owl jugs), which were made in England in slip ware. Bearbaiting was a popular sport in the English Midlands, and as late as 1830 a Catherine Dudley of Stoke Lane kept a bear which she hired for the purpose. The animal was attached to a pole by a ring through its nose, and dogs were loosed. Despite its handicap, the bear usually fought back with spirit.

The brothers Elers deserve particular mention. They came, originally, from a Saxon family, and gained their knowledge of the art of pottery in Cologne. They first settled in Holland before coming to England, and had worked as silversmiths. The noticeable influence of contemporary silver on some of the work attributed to them is, therefore, understandable (Plate 30).

The exact date on which they arrived in England is uncertain, but it was before 1693, and they transferred their activities to Staffordshire before 1698. This much is proved by a reference to them in 1698 by Dr. Martin Lister. Writing of a visit to the French porcelain factory at St. Cloud, Lister remarks:

'As for the Red ware of China, that has been, and is being done in England, to a far greater perfection than in China . . . and in this particular we are beholding to two Dutchmen Brothers who wrought in Staffordshire, and were not long since in Hammersmith.'

Hammersmith is a short distance from Fulham, and Lister, who was an acute observer, seems not to have heard of Dwight as a manufacturer of these wares.

The Elers found a suitable deposit of red clay at Bradwell Wood, in Staffordshire, which was exceptionally satisfactory, and manufacture appears to have been on a considerable scale. Apart from the red stoneware, it is difficult to say what they did make. Wedgwood, writing to Bentley in 1777, attributed the introduction of salt glazing in Staffordshire to the Elers, as well as the making of what he calls 'Chinese red Porcelain.' Wedgwood, who writes with an air of certainty, also refers to the casting of this body 'in plaster molds and turning it on the outside upon Lathes.' We may doubt the former, since the plaster mold was traditionally introduced into Staffordshire by Ralph Daniels of Cobridge in 1745, but of lathe turning there can be little doubt. Some examples attributed to the Elers are finished much too precisely to have been made in any other way.

It seems fairly certain, too, that the Elers brought salt glazing to Staffordshire, and, in the legal action already mentioned, David Elers admitted making 'brown muggs commonly called Cologne or stoneware.' It is, however, impossible to attribute anything of the kind to them with the slightest degree of certainty. It can fairly be said that, when the Elers came to Staffordshire, only peasant wares were being made. When they left, in 1710, the great modern industry in this region had made a beginning.

The quality of the wares made by the Elers, and their significance, did not pass unnoticed by others in Staffordshire. To protect their manufacturing secrets, the Elers employed only workmen of low intelligence wherever possible, and Astbury, by posing as an idiot, gained employment at the factory, and departed to make similar wares on his own account. Soon, red ware became a common item of manufacture, and it is difficult, more often than not, to separate the work of all the people making it.

At this point it would be as well to say that certain names are used very loosely in discussing the pottery of Staffordshire. Elers, Astbury, and Whieldon are examples of this. Wares made in the techniques presumably introduced by them are referred to as 'Elers' ware, 'Astbury' ware, or 'Whieldon' ware, but copying was commonplace, and technical knowledge, for the most part, common property. Such terms, therefore, cannot be regarded as exact without additional evidence in particular cases. Nevertheless, classification, which is essential to a discussion of pottery, would be difficult without so convenient a fiction, and it is, for this reason, entitled to remain.

Astbury made a great deal of red ware. He also perfected a white body, made by adding calcined flint, which he glazed with salt. This material could take a great deal of precise and intricate molding, and the thin glaze lent an added sharpness and clarity to the patterns. At first, stamped reliefs used by the Elers were continued, although such things as vine-leaf and grape ornament were often made separately and applied. Stamped reliefs on pads of clay, subsequently applied, are also to be seen. Following these, dishes and such things were made in metal molds, and later in molds of carved alabaster. Fired porous clay and plaster of Paris were also used for the same purpose.

Plaster of Paris was especially suitable for the process of slip casting. Liquid slip was poured into the hollow interior of the mold which was allowed to absorb some of the water. In this way a layer of firm clay was deposited on the plaster walls. The surplus was subsequently poured off, the mold removed, and the object left to dry to 'leather' hardness before firing. The same technique was used for forming some articles of porcelain, and it is commonly used today for intricate work, and for hollow ware which cannot be formed on the potter's wheel.

To this stage in development belong the dishes with elaborately molded and pierced ornament (Plate 46), ultimately derived from contemporary silver, which continued to be popular for many years. The same trend inspired the production of the teapot in such curious forms as that of a house, a kneeling camel, or a squirrel (Plate 41). Teapot designs in relief include the scallop (or pecten) shell, and molded representations of fantastic Chinese figures, which are a little unusual but appear on a number of things.

Chinoiseries became so popular on pottery and porcelain in molded and painted forms that it is desirable to discuss them here. I have already mentioned the popularity of Chinese porcelain in Europe, and this grew with the passing of time. Many illustrated books were published. Some were serious works written by travelers who had made the long and arduous journey to the East. Others were written and illustrated by men who had neither left Europe, nor studied the work of those who had acquired firsthand experience. Many of them were occupied in producing designs for decorative art of one kind or another. Boucher, for instance, did some work of the kind, and his *Suite de Figures Chinoises* inspired porcelain figures made by a number of European factories. Watteau, too, did some decoration of the kind for the Pavillon de la Muette, and Johann Gregor Höroldt, chief painter at the Meissen factory of Augustus the Strong, made engravings which were used by the factory as subjects to copy. The engraver, Jean Pillement, was also much copied, some of his work appearing in transfer-printed form on English porcelain.

The molded salt-glaze wares were followed by those decorated in enamel colors. About 1750 white salt-glazed stoneware from Staffordshire was being sent to Holland to be painted with enamels. The art is said to have been introduced into Staffordshire by two Dutchmen who settled in Hot Lane. The suggestion that one of them was named Willem Horologius is apocryphal, and nothing is known of them or their antecedents. The craft of enameling was certainly established in London a little before 1750. A studio had been established for this kind of work by William Duesbury, later founder of the Derby porcelain factory, by 1751, and white wares were sent to him for decoration by a number of porcelain factories. Whilst his hand on service ware cannot be identified, there is little doubt that the swans shown on Plate 31 were enameled by him.

By 1760 enameling was a common method of decorating salt-glazed ware, and plain, unmolded, specimens were being made for the purpose. Examples of the earlier molded wares painted with unrelated patterns are to be found, typical being certain rare teapots with scallop-shell molding, intended for Jacobite sympathizers, and having a small representation of Bonnie Prince Charlie above the shell.

Many of these painted wares have Chinese flowers in the *famille rose* palette, figure subjects in the Chinese manner being a good deal rarer. Portraits of Frederick the Great, a popular hero of the period in England, are quite often to be seen on teapots, dishes, and other things of the kind. England was allied to Prussia in the Seven Years' War, and such inscriptions as 'Success to the King of Prussia and his forces' exist. These specimens can be dated between 1756 and 1759 with some confidence.

A rich blue ground color is thought to have been introduced by William Littler, a salt-glaze potter who was a partner in the Longton Hall porcelain factory. This, called 'Littler's blue,' appears on fragments excavated from the site of the factory by Dr. Bernard Watney, and the traditional ascription was confirmed by them. This ground sometimes received the additional decoration of a little oil gilding, now mostly worn off, and slight enamel painting in white.

Transfer printing, further discussed on page 167, was quite frequently used. These specimens were done by Sadler & Green of Liverpool who, in 1756, swore an affidavit testifying to the fact that they had printed upwards of twelve hundred tiles in six hours, and had spent about seven years perfecting the process. These prints appear on salt-glazed ware in black, lilac, and red, and they are sometimes further embellished with enamels.

The surface of the almost white salt-glazed ware was particularly well-suited to enamel coloring, and the colors are often exceptionally brilliant in appearance. Standing apart from most of the examples discussed is the punch pot on plate 33 taken from an engraving which was also used as the subject of an early porcelain group from Bow. A certain Warner Edwards of Shelton is sometimes said to have been the first Staffordshire potter to use enamels on salt-glazed ware. An outside decorator, Mrs. Warburton, who was an early member of a family of potters which later became better known, enameled creamware for Wedgwood soon after 1760, and is also said to have decorated salt-glazed ware in the same way. Since Wedgwood seems to have been producing it at this time, the supposition is likely enough.

Most salt-glazed ware of this kind was made in Staffordshire, but, since it is unmarked, specimens cannot be referred to a factory of origin. To a lesser extent, both white and brown stoneware were made at Derby, and the two classes are mentioned in the *Derby Mercury* for 17th March, 1779, when the stock of the factory was offered for sale. In the early days of the Leeds factory, white salt-glazed ware was also manufactured, although specimens cannot be identified.

The figures made in Dwight's stoneware have already been mentioned. One or two rare examples of figures in red ware have been recorded, but these cannot be dated before about 1740. To Aaron Wood (a mold cutter, and member of the well-known Wood family of potters) has been attributed a series of unsophisticated models best represented by the so-called 'Pew' groups (Plate 40). These are two or three figures seated side by side on a high-backed oak settle. In the same spirit are figures of women in bell-shaped skirts. Some cats in 'marbled' clays ('agate' ware) are amusing, and recall much earlier cats in tin-enameled ware from London.

The earlier 'Pew' groups were hand-modeled, but busts of Maria Theresa and the Emperor, Francis I, in the Schreiber Collection (Victoria & Albert Museum) were made in molds, and mark the transition between the earlier things and the less interesting later figures inspired by the porcelain models of Meissen. Two of these, a Turk and Companion, are close copies of figures by J. F. Eberlein, and colored examples were probably painted by William Duesbury in London. His brilliantly colored swans are referred to in his account books as 'Swiming swans donn all over.' These seem to owe something to the Meissen Swan service, and a figure of a dog sold in London some years ago amusingly underlined this practice of copying from Meissen, since it bore on its collar the initials MPM – *Meissner Porzellan Manufaktur*. It is doubtful whether the potters recognized this significance. A few figures in salt glaze also appear in porcelain. In particular, an arbor group was repeated closely at Longton Hall, and the Eberlein *Turk and Companion* were done here, and at Bow. The latter were originally based on illustrations in the *Différentes Nations du Levant* by de Ferriol, published in Paris in 1714, which was used at Meissen as a source of inspiration for figure models.

A distinct class of ware made from about 1740 to 1776 is the so-called 'scratch blue.' Both dates and inscriptions are common. The designs, usually floral, were incised into the body of the ware and colored with powdered cobalt blue before firing. Most specimens are either mugs or jugs, but a large loving cup is illustrated on Plate 43.

Most of the 18th century salt-glazed wares have no Continental counterparts, and, for this reason, are particularly English in feeling. Generally, forgeries are few, although some plain specimens have been decorated with enamels at a later date. Most frequently reproduced are the brown-glazed wares with applied reliefs, which were again popular during the 19th century.

30. TEAPOT. RED STONEWARE. STAFFORDSHIRE. C. 1700

11 cm. The Victoria and Albert Museum, London

One of the few specimens which can be attributed to the Elers with safety. It is partly based on a silver pattern (the faceted form, for instance) and partly on Yi Hsing stoneware. On the base is a pseudo-Chinese mark in relief. The molded decoration in the panels is heightened by the use of a dull gold background which is particularly effective in conjunction with the dark red body. The animal forming the knop has been copied from a Chinese original.

31. SWANS WITH CYGNETS. SALT-GLAZED WARE STAFFORDSHIRE. C. 1750

20.5 cm. The British Museum, London

The coloring of these brilliantly enameled swans seems to be the work of William Duesbury at his London studio. They appear in his account book as 'swiming swans donn all over,' and were sent to London from Staffordshire for this purpose. The model was probably derived in the first place from the 'Swan' service, made at Meissen to the order of Augustus III for the director, Count von Brühl, in 1737. Somewhat similar swans appear among the table appointments of this service, but the coloring is entirely original.

32. TEAPOT. SALT GLAZE WARE. STAFFORDSHIRE. 1755

10.5 cm. The Syndics of the Fitzwilliam Museum, Cambridge

This teapot, which has a twig handle and spout, is decorated with vine leaves and grapes joined by vine stems. The colors do not appear to be those of Duesbury, and were probably applied in Staffordshire.

33. PUNCH POT. SALT GLAZE WARE. STAFFORDSHIRE. C. 1760

21 cm. The Victoria and Albert Museum (Schreiber Collection), London

This punch pot, looking like an outsize teapot, was used for the making and serving of punch, a blend of spirits with hot milk, spices, and sugar. Punch was extremely popular, and large bowls were also used in its preparation and service. The decoration in enamel colors is a little sketchy, and has obviously been suggested by an engraving. The subject, *Lovers with a Birdcage*, was also used at Bow about 1750 for an extremely fine group by the Muses Modeler.

30

31

32

33

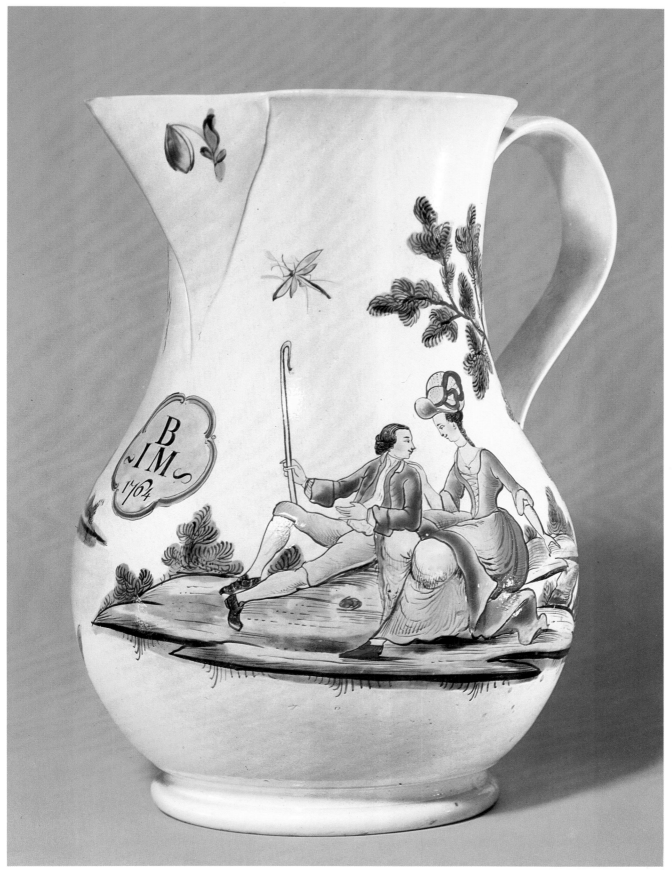

34

34. JUG. SALT GLAZE WARE. STAFFORDSHIRE. 1764

20.5 cm. The Victoria and Albert Museum (Wallace Elliot Bequest), London

This jug is amusingly decorated in enamel colors, the subject being a gallant and a lady masquerading as a shepherd and shepherdess. These pastoral masquerades did not become so fashionable in England as they were on the Continent, although the subject is quite often to be seen in porcelain in one version or another. The inscription on this jug is as follows:

B

IM

1764.

The initials, presumably, are those of the person for whom it was made.

35. ALE BOTTLE. DWIGHT'S STONEWARE. C. 1680

20.5 cm. The Victoria and Albert Museum (Schreiber Collection), London

This bottle was found in a walled-up room in the old Fulham pottery in 1862, and is, therefore, undoubtedly from this source. In form and glaze it closely resembles the Rhineland stoneware bottles (*Bartmannkrüge*) popular in England at the time. The C R to be noted in the medallion stands for *Carolus Rex*, in this case Charles II. The mask differs noticeably from German prototypes. These 17th century English copies of Rhineland stoneware are extremely rare, but it is possible that some are misattributed to German sources in English private collections.

36. PRINCE RUPERT. DWIGHT'S STONEWARE. C. 1680

57.5 cm. The British Museum, London

Portrait bust of Prince Rupert of Bavaria (1619–1682), son of Frederick V, Elector Palatine and King of Bohemia, and Princess Elizabeth of England. Rupert supported Charles I during the Civil War, and later joined Charles II at Versailles, returning to England at the Reformation. He was a member of the Board of Trade, and helped to found the Hudson's Bay Company. This superb portrait is one of the most important of English ceramic achievements. Modeled directly in the stoneware body by Grinling Gibbons, it was fired as it left the sculptor's hand, and no molds were taken by which it could be duplicated. It is, for this reason, unique. The only decoration is a little gilding.

37. HUNTSMAN. DWIGHT'S STONEWARE. C. 1680

24.5 cm. The British Museum, London

This finely modeled figure in grayish stoneware has been attributed to the English sculptor and wood carver, Grinling Gibbons. It is unique. The huntsman carries a hare slung over his right shoulder, and a sword at his side. The slight defect noticeable on the face was done whilst the figure was still plastic, probably when it was being placed in the kiln (see Plate 36).

36

38

39

42

43

44

45

46

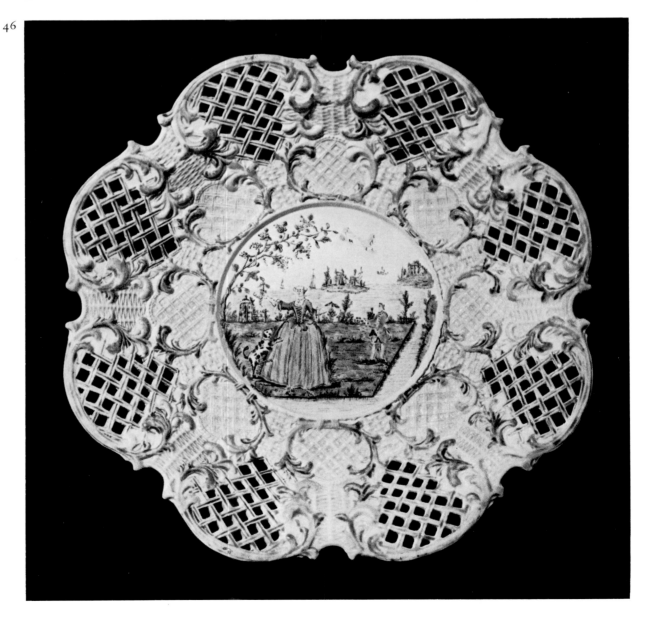

38. TANKARD. FULHAM STONEWARE. 1739

25.5 cm. The Victoria and Albert Museum (Schreiber Collection), London

A late but imposing example of Fulham stoneware in the Rhineland tradition. These were not, apparently, made until after Dwight's death. The decoration was molded separately and applied, and represents huntsmen and hounds pursuing a hare. The following inscriptions are incised into the body:

Between the reliefs

Southwell for Ever. C.W.M. 1739.

Under the base

John Harwell.

Mugs and tankards of this kind were often reproduced subsequently.

---

39. MUG. SALT GLAZE WARE. STAFFORDSHIRE. 1740

18 cm. The Victoria and Albert Museum (Schreiber Collection), London

This mug, decorated with stamped and applied reliefs, commemorates the taking of Portobello by Admiral Vernon. The decoration represents the battle, with a relief of the Admiral, in addition to ships, buildings, cannon, and so forth. The inscription reads:

The British Glory : Reviv:d by Admiral Vernon :

He took Porto Bel (lo) with six :: ships only :

Nov ye: 22 1739.

Similar reliefs occur on Astbury ware.

---

40. GROUP. SALT GLAZE WARE. STAFFORDSHIRE. C. 1740

19 cm. The Syndics of the Fitzwilliam Museum, Cambridge

This is related to the so-called 'Pew' groups, both in the style of modeling, and in the high-backed bench which resembles a pew. It represents the perenially popular subject of The Fall, Eve presumably, despite the greater height, being on the right of the illustration. The fig leaves are summarily indicated, whilst the reader may, perhaps, wonder at the appearance of flowers and apples on the tree at the same time. The eyes are indicated with almost black clay. Groups of this kind were modeled individually, and not reproduced from molds. They are extremely rare.

---

41. TEAPOT. SALT GLAZE WARE. STAFFORDSHIRE. C. 1745

14.5 cm. The Syndics of the Fitzwilliam Museum, Cambridge

This teapot in the form of a squirrel holding a nut is related to other salt-glazed teapots in the form of camels, houses, and so forth, but it is considerably rarer. They are all light in weight, and slipcast. The handle is in the form of a dragon, and the molded decoration of birds amid branches is ultimately derived from Chinese painted decoration.

42. ARBOR GROUP. SALT GLAZE WARE. STAFFORDSHIRE. C. 1745

18 cm. The Brighton Art Gallery and Museum (Willett Collection), Brighton, Sussex

This amusing salt-glazed group of lovers under a fan-shaped arbor is typical of the whole group. It was slipcast with a certain amount of hand-modeling. The eyes are indicated with brown clay. Specimens are now exceedingly rare.

---

43. LOVING CUP. SALT GLAZE WARE. STAFFORDSHIRE. 1748

20 cm. Brighton Art Gallery and Museum (Willett Collection), Brighton, Sussex

A large loving cup with strap handles decorated with incised concentric circles. The inscription reads:

Elizabeth Wall 1748

George Wall 1748

and is touched with blue. This example belongs to the so-called 'scratched blue' class.

---

44. CANDLESTICK. SALT GLAZE WARE. STAFFORDSHIRE. C. 1750

28.5 cm. The Syndics of the Fitzwilliam Museum, Cambridge

The gnarled tree stump is surmounted by a foliate socket, and the flowers and leaves are separately modeled and applied. The stag at the base resembles a Meissen 'stag' tureen of about 1750 (cf. catalogue of the Fischer Collection, No. 585, page 85). The material is a very pale buff in color.

---

45. TEAPOT. SALT GLAZE WARE. STAFFORDSHIRE. C. 1750

12 cm. The Brighton Art Gallery and Museum (Willett Collection), Brighton, Sussex

This teapot has a crabstock handle and spout, based on twig forms. The decoration is carried out in green, blue, puce, and yellow enamels, the rose being colored with a white pigment similar to the white tin enamel used in the making of delftware. The subject is a half-length portrait of Prince Charles Edward, the Young Pretender, in Scottish dress, within a laurel wreath flanked by a rose and a thistle, the significance of which is discussed in the text (page 74). This teapot was made for Jacobite sympathizers, and the enameling may have been done in Holland. Certainly, after the bloody defeat of the 1745 Rebellion, England was no longer a particularly safe place for adherents of the House of Stuart.

46. DISH. SALT GLAZE WARE. STAFFORDSHIRE. C. 1760

27.5 cm. The Victoria and Albert Museum (Schreiber Collection), London

This dish is molded in imitation of basketwork, with pierced trellis panels. It is based on a contemporary silver pattern, as were so many salt-glazed dishes of the kind. The center is painted with a lady picking grapes beside a canal, with an estuary in the background. The enamels are principally pink, green, turquoise, light blue, and yellow, and the *rococo* scroll-work is picked out in colors. The treatment of the subject suggests Dutch enameling. Pierced work became more general with the introduction of creamware, and, towards the end of the century, was most elaborate (cf. Plate 62).

THE CONNECTION between Astbury and the Elers has already been mentioned. John Astbury, and his son, Thomas, were making pottery in Staffordshire in 1725, and other members of the family appear in later 18th century records. The early wares are unmarked, but some red ware of a later date, probably made about 1760, has the mark 'Astbury' impressed, and similar marks appear on isolated specimens of black 'basaltes' and creamware.

The red ware was, of course, derived from Astbury's period of employment with the Elers, and he used a similar body for a ware decorated with stamped ornament on applied white clay pads, the whole being covered with a yellowish lead glaze. The body varies in color from red to pale buff, but this is partly due to firing temperature rather than to variations in the body itself.

The applied clay pads were traditionally made from white Devon clay, and Astbury is said to have been the first to use clay from this source. This is somewhat doubtful. The discovery of this clay is also attributed to William Cookworthy of Plymouth at a much later date. Additionally, flint burned and crushed to powder, first suggested by Dwight of Fulham, was probably introduced by Astbury. This is an essential ingredient of the creamware body.

The dating of this class of ware is greatly assisted by a bowl made in 1739 decorated with reliefs of views of Portobello, ships, sailors, and guns, which has this inscription:

> Ye Prid(e) of Spain humbled by Admiral Vernon
> He took Portobello with six ships only
> Nov ye 22 1739.

A salt-glazed version appears on Plate 39, and it is unlikely that most things decorated in this way were made before 1740.

Another kind of molded decoration is provided by vine leaves and grapes, often in white on a dark ground, which became extremely popular, and this *motif* is used on a variety of wares. A colored salt-glaze version appears on Plate 32. Like the Elers, Astbury based many of his forms on contemporary silver, and such things as paw-feet to teapots and the like are obvious silver patterns.

Astbury made a certain amount of 'agate' ware. The clays of different colors were first laid in slabs, one on the other, which were then repeatedly divided and subdivided until they had mingled sufficiently. Work of a similar appearance, in which colored slips were intermingled, is referred to as 'marbled.' Use was often made of clays stained with blue and brown for this kind of work, which was also done in France at Apt and elsewhere.

Later red wares attributed to the Astbury family are often decorated with engineturning. This was done by cutting the patterns on a lathe before firing, and they often take the form of a kind of basketwork. The method was much used by Wedgwood for decorating red ware, called by him *rosso antico*, and for his black 'basaltes' ware.

Some of the early Staffordshire figures have been attributed to Astbury. These are in the red, brown, and white clays which were used for the other wares described, in combination with a lead glaze, and in some cases the glaze is splashed with color. The latter are often referred to 'Astbury-Whieldon,' because Thomas Whieldon, later discussed, made much use of dappled glazes, and an attribution to Astbury is uncertain. These Astbury figures are unsophisticated, and obviously an amusing form of peasant pottery. Some are repetitions of models which also appear in an early salt-glazed version. Most surviving examples are of horsemen and musicians, and they are extremely rare. Some musicians are illustrated on Plate 48.

Thomas Whieldon, born in 1719, established a factory at Fenton Low, in Staffordshire, for the making of such small items as knife handles in 'agate' ware in 1740. His factory was very small, consisting of a row of thatched cottages. He sold his own products, traveling from town to town with samples of his wares.

Whieldon was not only influential for the wares he made, but for his connection with other potters who were later to become important in the history of this great Staffordshire industry. In April, 1749, for instance, he 'hired Siah Spode to give him from this time to Martelmas next 2/3 d., or 2/6d. if he deserves it.' Josiah Spode was later to introduce the formula for making bone china, now the standard porcelain body. In 1754 Whieldon met Josiah Wedgwood and entered into partnership with him. It is upon Wedgwood that we depend for much information about Whieldon's personal character, and the former held him in high esteem. Whieldon agreed with his new partner that Wedgwood should experiment with colored glazes, which were to be used for their mutual benefit, but Whieldon laid no claim to the secret of these colors. The experiments led to the production of wares molded in the form of cauliflowers, pineapples, and the like, covered with green and yellow glazes of a quality never before seen from Staffordshire. An early Wedgwood teapot of a type made by him about this time appears on Plate 81.

The early Whieldon wares were made in a light buff body, and the glaze was mottled with the purplish-brown derived from manganese oxide, the technique being somewhat similar to that used by Bernard Palissy on the reverse of many of his dishes. Later, other coloring oxides – green, gray, and yellow – were used in conjunction with manganese to give a mottled, or 'clouded,' effect, which is referred to as 'tortoiseshell' (see Plate 51). These 'tortoise-shell' glazes are the commonest survivals, and were used to cover a variety of wares – plates, teapots, coffeepots, creamers, and so forth. Many such things had molded decoration, and those based on silver are the most frequently to be noted. Even *chinoiseries*, molded on faceted teapots, are to be seen occasionally. Floral and vine-leaf moldings are extremely effective.

The control which Whieldon had attained over his material is proved by the existence of wares with double walls (Plate 62), the outer wall pierced with a fairly elaborate pattern. The diversity of his production can be seen from excavations on the site of the old factory at Fenton Low, where shards of hard red ware similar to that of Astbury, salt-glazed pottery (including some of the 'scratched-blue, class), black-glazed ware of the kind attributed to Jackfield, and a buff-colored ware which is an early version of Wedgwood's creamware, were all found. Whieldon made frequent use of the 'crabstock' handle and spout to such things as teapots. These imitated twigs, and covers to teapots were often in the form of a bird with outstretched wings.

Figures decorated with these colored glazes were made, and most are naive and amusing. A few appear both in this medium, and in salt-glazed ware, and some are also to be seen in a heavily glazed white porcelain made during the first years of the Longton Hall factory – the so-called 'Snowman' group, later discussed. Whieldon called these figures 'image toys,' and they range from fairly close copies of Chinese figures originally in the white porcelain of Tê Hua (Fukien Province) known as *blanc de Chine*, to birds imitated from contemporary porcelain on *rococo* tree-branch bases. The latter were made about 1760, and the mottled glaze covering is very decorative. Whieldon figures vary in date from 1750, or a little before, to about 1780, and they show an increasing degree of sophistication in modeling and finish with the advancing years. (Compare Plates 58 and 65, for instance.)

Whieldon had great influence over the growth of the industry in Staffordshire, particularly during the middle years of the 18th century. In so doing, he became rich, and was made High Sheriff of the County in 1786. He died in 1798 at the age of 79.

The black-glazed ware found on the site of Whieldon's factory was made elsewhere in Staffordshire, and particularly at a factory in Shropshire, at Jackfield. It has been the custom to attribute all black-glazed ware to Jackfield indiscriminately, but, in fact, only a few fairly well-defined types seem to have been made here. The date on which the factory was established is unknown, but about 1750 it was under the direction of Maurice Thursfield. The black glaze was applied over a red body, and decorated, often with Jacobite emblems, in oil gilding and lacquer (i. e. unfired) colors. For the most part, these are now in poor condition. Since they were not fired they soon yielded to daily wear and tear. Of the wares commonly attributed to this factory, it can only be said that a Staffordshire origin, and, in particular, the factory of Whieldon, is the more likely for many of them.

A word needs to be said on the Jacobites, because *motifs* associated with them appear frequently on English pottery and glass of the period, and, less often, on porcelain.

The name is given to followers of the House of Stuart after the Revolution of 1688 which unseated James II from the English throne, and replaced him with William, Prince of Orange. It comes from Jacobus, the Latin form of James. The Stuarts had many adherents, principally in Scotland, but also, it would seem, in Staffordshire, and in the Midlands generally. A Jacobite revolt took place in 1715, and another in 1745 when Bonnie Prince Charlie landed in Scotland and proclaimed his father James III. He was bloodily defeated at Culloden by the Duke of Cumberland, the second son of George II, who received the soubriquet of 'The Butcher' for his treatment of the rebels. The fact remains, however, that this was the last Jacobite rebellion, and henceforward they played a diminishing part in English politics, although the present English Queen is known as Mrs. Philip Mountbatten to a few hardy survivors on the lunatic fringe.

Apart from occasional portraits, such as the one shown on Plate 45, roses are a Jacobite emblem. A large rose is sometimes said to stand for the Old Pretender to the throne, James Francis Edward Stuart, and two buds, where present, for his sons, Charles Edward (Bonnie Prince Charlie) who was the Young Pretender, and Henry Benedict, the youngest. The supposition is a little doubtful, and another suggestion that the rose may actually symbolize the disputed crown, and the buds the Old and Young Pretenders, is, perhaps, more acceptable. The oak leaf is also a Jacobite emblem, and may symbolize a new Restoration, similar to that of Charles II who hid in the Boscobel oak – sometimes commemorated on slip ware. The thistle, of course, represents the Crown of Scotland, and this, too, may have one or two buds.

The House of Hanover was far from being seated firmly on the English throne during the 18th century, and many notable people, Dr. Samuel Johnson for instance, were sympathizers with the Stuart cause. It is, therefore, not surprising to find oblique references of this kind on pottery and related things.

THE FIGURES DISCUSSED hitherto have been, for the most part, by-products of the manufacture of use-ful wares. The first pottery figures to be produced on a fairly large scale were those of Ralph Wood.
Wood was a member of an important family of potters in Staffordshire. He was born in 1715, the son of Ralph Wood, a miller, of Burslem. Two years later his brother, Aaron Wood, was born, and the attribution of the salt-glazed 'Pew' groups to the latter has already been mentioned.

Both Ralph and Aaron Wood seem to have started as 'block-cutters,' that is, as makers of molds, and signed 'blocks' for molding salt-glazed wares have survived from both of them. The exact date on which Ralph Wood founded his factory is unknown, but 1745 is, perhaps, a legitimate supposition. Few surviving figures can be attributed to a date earlier than 1760, and manufacture continued until about 1790. His son, also Ralph Wood, was born in 1748, and joined his father in the family business, probably before 1770. The father died in 1772, and the son in 1795.

Figures made by the Woods are frequently marked. Two marks are to be seen – 'R. Wood' and 'Ra. Wood,' and the town, 'Burslem,' is sometimes added to both. These differences are used to separate the work of the father and the son, the latter using 'Ra. Wood.' There are a number of reasons why this assumption appears to be valid, the most convincing being that all known figures marked 'R. Wood' are decorated with colored glazes. These are not in the Whieldon tradition of intermingled, or 'tortoise-shell,' colors. Instead, each glaze is reasonably distinct and separate. Some of the 'Ra. Wood' figures, on the other hand, are colored with enamels over a clear glaze. A factory number, too, is some-times added to pieces of the type associated with the son, but never to those done in the technique associated with the father. An unusual example by the son appears on Plate 145. This is a group of a kind which is not uncommon in the creamware body used by them, but, in this case, it is in porcelain, and decorated with enamel colors.

Perhaps associated with the Woods was a modeler from France, named Jean Voyez, whose work was distinctly influenced by that of Paul-Louis Cyfflé of Lunéville. Voyez is reputed to have come from the Amiens district, and soon after 1760 was in London working as a silversmith, and subsequently as a wood carver for the Adam Brothers. He was brought to the notice of Josiah Wedgwood, then seeking modelers of talent, who was told that Voyez was reputed the best modeler in London. Wedg-wood gave him a contract for three years in 1768, and advanced money for his journey to Staffordshire. This arrangement, however, was short-lived. Voyez was sentenced to three months' imprisonment and a flogging in 1769 at the Staffordshire Assizes for an unspecified offence. It is said that he was dis-covered modeling from the nude, the model being the daughter of Wedgwood's coachman.

Whatever the cause, it is certain that it cannot have been lack of ability, because Wedgwood undertook to pay him his full wages of thirty-six shillings a week, provided he did not work elsewhere in Staffordshire. Dissatisfied with this arrangement, Voyez took employment with Wedgwood's imitator, Palmer of Hanley, and spread reports detrimental to Wedgwood.

We know little of his connection with the Woods, although he shared lodgings with Ralph Wood Junior in Burslem for a time. His presence has been inferred, principally on grounds of style, and from jugs decorated in the manner of Ralph Wood with a relief decoration, and inscribed 'Fair Hebe' (Plate 71), some of which are signed by Voyez. Figures in the style of this jug can also be assigned to Voyez with some certainty.

The figures made at the time in the style of Cyfflé (Plate 67, for instance) argue the presence of a French modeler. These figures are in a pleasantly sentimental vein, and Cyfflé liked such subjects as a cobbler whistling to a bird in a cage (a play on his own name), and things of the kind. These were made between 1766 and 1777, and it seems unlikely that anything derived from his work could have been made in Staffordshire much before 1770. The figure of the boy as a chimney sweep (Plate 67), first modeled by Cyfflé, appears as a Wood model, and was probably the work of Voyez.

The finest work associated with Ralph Wood the elder is an equestrian figure of *Hudibras* (Plate 52), after an engraving by Hogarth, which may have been modeled by Aaron Wood. An amusing group called *The Vicar and Moses*, in which the parson sleeps soundly in his pulpit, oblivious to the droning voice of his clerk praying windily below him, is shown on Plate 66. This was extremely popular, and later repeated by Enoch Wood and others. Another remarkably fine group is that of *Charity*, a woman standing with children, which was made in several versions. Animal figures include stags and hinds, goats, sheep, and rams, many copied from models made by the porcelain factories, and the style of the latter is also to be seen in some of the Wood figures and groups.

Useful wares which can be identified include vases decorated in colored glazes; a flower holder in the form of a dolphin is an example. Both decorative and useful was the Toby jug, a peculiarly English concept, a Whieldon example of which appears on Plate 63. They are beer jugs, and usually take the form of a man seated, although at least one woman, Martha Gunn the gin woman, who is said to have taught George III to swim, is known. The crown of the hat (when it still exists) is detachable, and forms a cup. A few examples have inscriptions – 'It is all out, then fill him agian' is an example.

The origin of the Toby jug has been much disputed. Some would like to see in him a reference to Uncle Toby from Sterne's *Tristram Shandy*, first published in 1759; others, to a character in a song, *The Brown Jug*, who was called Toby Philpot. This appeared in 1761, and engravings of Toby Philpot were popular. The origin of this kind of thing is much older. The *rhyton*, a drinking cup in human form, was a *jeu d'esprit* of Greek potters of the 5th century B.C., and the fragment of an English medieval jug shown on Plate 8 is in the same tradition.

The first Toby jugs were made by Whieldon in the characteristic mottled glazes, and an example of the kind is illustrated on Plate 63. The evolution of the Toby, however, owes much to Ralph Wood, and his work was subsequently imitated. The same molds were used by the son for jugs decorated in enamel colors.

There are many variations on the early models. The *Night Watchman*, for instance, holds a lantern in his right hand. The *Drunken Parson* is a theme repeated in the group shown on Plate 70, depicting a parson being steered home with difficulty by his clerk. *Lord Howe* commemorated the victory over the French off Ushant in 1794. Tobies were made by many Staffordshire potters during the 18th century, and continued to be popular during the 19th.

Another member of the Wood family to make figures was Enoch Wood of Burslem, the son of Aaron Wood, who was born in 1759. He worked for a time, whilst still a boy, for Josiah Wedgwood, and was later apprenticed to Palmer of Hanley. He joined Ralph Wood Junior in partnership in 1783, but later founded Enoch Wood & Co., the style of which was changed almost at once to Wood & Caldwell, James Caldwell being taken into partnership in 1790. The style, Enoch Wood & Sons, was adopted in 1818.

Enoch Wood showed considerable skill as a modeler from an early age, a plaque in the British Museum with a shield of arms and floral decoration being done at the age of twelve years. At eighteen he modeled a plaque, based on the jasper ware of Wedgwood, which was copied from the *Descent from the Cross* by Rubens. He achieved some local success, too, with a portrait bust of John Wesley, the revivalist preacher. His skill is here shown by the portrait bust of himself on Plate 74, – the only surviving portrait of the kind of an 18th century manufacturer, with the exception of some rare jasper medallions of Wedgwood.

Enoch Wood made many figures and groups of excellent quality, although some were derivative. That of the actor, said to be James Quin, as *Falstaff* was undoubtedly taken from the Bow and Derby models. The group of *St. George and the Dragon* was derived from the same subject by Ralph Wood, and the *Bacchus and Ariadne* (originally by Houdon) was copied from Wedgwood. Perhaps the most striking of the Enoch Wood models is the large figure of *Eloquence*, sometimes said to be *St. Paul preaching to the Athenians*, illustrated on Plate 72.

Apart from figures, Enoch Wood made all kinds of ware current in Staffordshire at the time, but most are unimportant artistically.

THE WARES OF JOSIAH WEDGWOOD

THE WORK OF JOSIAH Wedgwood had a profound and far-reaching effect, not only on the subsequent course of pottery and porcelain manufacture in England, but also on Continental wares. The name of Wedgwood is, in fact, one of the most influential in the later history of the ceramic art.

Josiah Wedgwood was born in 1730, the youngest of thirteen children. His father, Thomas Wedgwood, belonged to a family already well known in Staffordshire as makers of pottery, and Aaron, Richard, and Thomas Wedgwood of Burslem were cited as defendants in Dwight's action of 1693.

Wedgwood's father died in 1739, and, at the age of nine, Josiah was sent to help in a factory belonging to his brother, Thomas. In 1751 he became a partner with John Harrison of Newcastle (Staffs.) but this arrangement proved to be unsatisfactory, and he entered partnership with Whieldon in 1754 as I have already recorded. This partnership was fruitful, but Whieldon was not sufficiently enterprising, and, in 1759, Wedgwood left to start in business on his own account at the Ivy House Works in Burslem.

Here, Wedgwood first turned his attention to perfecting the kind of body which had been used by Whieldon as a base for his work in colored glazes. The earliest attempts were deep cream in color, which was hardly pleasing, but within a short time this defect had been overcome, and, in 1765, Wedgwood presented a dinner service of creamware to Queen Charlotte, who gave him permission to call it 'Queen's Ware.' By 1774 the new earthenware had become so well known that Wedgwood was asked to make a service for Catherine the Great of Russia, consisting of 952 pieces painted with different English views. This caused Wedgwood some anxiety lest his account for the work be unpaid. His fears were not entirely groundless, since a sumptuous service and table decoration ordered from Sèvres in the year following were never finally paid for. Catherine sent a small amount on account, and the Foreign Ministers of both countries became involved in subsequent attempts to collect the balance.

The Wedgwood service was made for the Palace of La Grenouillière in the Tsarkoe Selo, St. Petersburg, and a green frog was painted on each piece. It is now in Leningrad, but a few pieces exist in England (Plate 82), and others were painted without the frog, including a small tea service.

Creamware was used for a large variety of purposes, even for tiles for lining the walls of the bathroom. It made an immediate appeal because of its clean, simple, shapes (Plate 83). The decoration was frequently transfer-printed by Sadler & Green of Liverpool, but quite often it had such borders as the ivy leaf and berry, the Greek fret, the egg and dart, and the anthemion (honeysuckle) in simple colors. When more elaborate painting was required Wedgwood probably gave the work to independent decorators, such as Robinson & Rhodes of Leeds. He also opened a painting studio in Chelsea, where the 'Frog' service for Catherine was done.

Ware to be transfer-printed was sent to Liverpool by pack horse, and work of this kind was done outside the factory until about 1800.

Wedgwood also made vases of creamware which were decorated by 'marbling,' and a certain amount of 'agate' ware was among his earliest production, as well as such standard wares as salt-glazed stoneware which was soon discontinued.

For some years Wedgwood labored to perfect a black stoneware, and, about 1768, he produced a fine-grained black body which was hard enough to be worked and polished on the lapidary's wheel. This he termed 'black porcelaine,' or 'basaltes' ware. A black ware known as 'Egyptian black' had occasionally been made in Staffordshire before this date, and it is supposed to have been known to the Elers. Wedgwood, however, perfected it, and used it first for wares painted in red and white with what he called 'encaustic' enamels in imitation of Greek vases which had been found in Etruscan tombs, and were therefore assumed to be Italian (Plate 75). The same misapprehension caused him to name his new factory 'Etruria.' This, about two miles from Burslem, he occupied in 1768, and in the same year formed a new and fruitful partnership with Thomas Bentley, which lasted until the latter's death in 1780.

Bentley spent most of his time in London, and Wedgwood's correspondence with him is a rich mine of information about the progress of the factory.

The manufacture of red stoneware went on under the name of *rosso antico*, and it was also used in conjunction with the black body. This ware was not a favorite with Wedgwood, and it was not made in large quantities. From about 1770 the 'basaltes' ware was used for large busts of classical and modern authors and the like, principally for library decoration, and vases were soon a popular item of manufacture. Demand, in fact, so far outran supply that John Coward (a wood carver who worked for the Adam Brothers) was engaged to fix black wood bases, tops, and the like, to defective specimens. Wedgwood wrote to Bentley:

'He has patched up some and bronzed others of the invalids, & sold them, & serves the old cream colour and gilt ones in the same way, & we have doctered, I won't say Tinkered, near £100 worth of what we deem'd reprobates here, & by next weeks end I believe shall not have a single waster left.'

A certain amount of trouble was experienced in getting applied relief decoration to adhere to the curved surface of vases and similar things, but these difficulties were overcome about 1775, and the earlier plain engineturning and flutings were superseded by more elaborately molded reliefs. Plaques with reliefs of classical subjects were a popular item of manufacture, and oval medallions with portraits of notabilities, ancient and modern, were sold in large numbers.

It is difficult to say when Wedgwood first conceived his idea of the jasper ware which was his most original and successful discovery. Undoubtedly he was inspired by the *biscuit* porcelain of Sèvres which, soon after 1770, was being imitated by the English porcelain factories at Chelsea and Derby. But the jasper body was something quite new, containing barium sulphate from Derbyshire, and although it resembled *biscuit* porcelain to some extent, it must certainly be classified as an unglazed stoneware. The history of its development is set forth in Wedgwood's letters to Bentley about this time. By 1774 most of the initial difficulties appear to have been overcome, and, in January, 1775, Wedgwood wrote:

'The blue body I am likewise absolute in of almost any shade, & have likewise a beautiful Sea Green, and several other colors for grounds to Cameos, Intaglios, &c.'

The first manufacture was colored throughout the body, but this was presently changed to a wash of color *over* it, the two varieties being known as 'solid' and 'dip.'

Most jasper has a light blue ground with decoration applied in white relief. The variations usually preserve this basic arrangement, and differences are generally of background color. Apart from the light blue and sea green, Wedgwood introduced dark blue, lavender, sage green, lilac, olive green, and yellow, although the last is extremely rare. Additionally, a black jasper is sometimes to be seen which needs carefully to be distinguished from the black 'basaltes,' and an intense bluish black was used for Wedgwood's copy of the 'Portland' vase. Although a combination of two colors is the more usual, occasional examples in three or more colors are to be seen. Jasper was never glazed, but about 1780 a waxen gloss was given to a few examples. These are distinctly rare. Most jasper has a slight gloss, mainly due to the polishing of a very finegrained stoneware, and it was the custom to have the relief work of the more important specimens undercut by lapidaries. Reliefs on later examples tend to become shallower.

The first use of jasper was for cameos 'with figures and heads in our fine white composition,' as well as seals and the like. The larger plaques were, presumably, being made by April, 1775, and candlesticks are mentioned in a letter of this date. These larger items, however, were extremely troublesome in the early stages, and the application of reliefs to a curved surface, necessary for the manufacture of vases, was not possible until after 1780. The exact date on which the first jasper vases were made is not known, but it may have been as late as 1785. After this date, however, such things were produced in considerable quantities, as well as ornamental tea ware and similar curved items.

The most important work done by Wedgwood in jasper was his copy of the 'Portland' vase (Plate 53) which was lent to him for the purpose by the Duke of Portland. The work occupied about four years, from 1786 to 1790, the copy being pronounced accurate by none other than Sir Joshua Reynolds, P.R.A. Another vase, which was highly regarded by Wedgwood himself, is decorated with a subject sometimes called the *Apotheosis of Homer* (Plate 54). Relatively few freestanding figures were done, either in 'basaltes' or jasper, although the distinguished cane-ware portrait of Voltaire shown on Plate 80 was also repeated in 'basaltes' ware. Most figures, however, are applied to vases and the like, or support candleholders. The earlier fashion for figures as table decoration was beginning to wane. Most existing jasper figures are in white, mounted on a colored jasper pedestal.

The greater part of production was given to plaques, medallions, and cameos. The larger plaques, both 'basaltes' and jasper, were used to inset in chimney pieces, in articles of furniture, and the like. They can, in fact, occasionally be seen in French furniture of the late Louis Seize period, replacing the plaques of Sèvres porcelain which had been exclusively used hitherto. Among the furniture ornamented in this way may be numbered cabinets and *commodes* of all kinds, and even the grand pianoforte, then being introduced.

The oval portrait medallions (Plate 78) were a fashionable product. They include excellent likenesses of such notable people as George III and Queen Charlotte; the Admirals Nelson, Keppel, and Howe; writers such as Chaucer and Shakespeare; actors like Garrick; scientists like Sir Isaac Newton and Linnaeus; and others. Many special subjects were done for Continental customers, one such consignment for Leopold II, Holy Roman Emperor from 1790 to 1792, being invoiced in 1790. Leopold was, at this time, allied with England.

In the classical series of medallions were included portraits of illustrious persons of Asia, Egypt, and Greece. Statesmen, philosophers, poets, and emperors were among those represented. The Emperors were done in a set of fifty-two from Nerva to Constantine – and these were followed by the Popes, the Kings and Queens of England, and the Kings of France.

Among the modelers employed by Wedgwood for this kind of work may be numbered such important artists as John Flaxman, R.A. The latter was the son of a molder who had already supplied Wedgwood with casts from the antique, and the younger Flaxman, a notable exponent of neo-classicism, did much relief work of the kind, including the *Apotheosis of Homer* already mentioned. In 1787 Flaxman went to Rome, whence he continued to correspond with Wedgwood. William Hackwood was principal modeler from 1769 to 1830, and did much work in the neo-classical style, as well as some of the portrait reliefs. Wedgwood permitted him to sign a few examples of his work – a very rare privilege. James Tassie, whose wax portraits in relief are well-known, also supplied Wedgwood with models, and the sculptor, John Bacon R.A., sent models to Etruria. It seems to have been a fashionable pursuit to design for Wedgwood. Both Lady Templewood and Lady Diana Beauclerk were happy to do work of the kind. George Stubbs, the well-known animal painter, not only executed a large family portrait in oils, but he modeled the *Fall of Phaeton* and some reliefs of horses.

The success of Wedgwood's various ornamental and useful wares was such that he had many contemporary imitators in Staffordshire. Humphrey Palmer, who employed Voyez, was the first, but he was soon followed by Adams of Greengates, whose blue jasper is exceptionally good. John Turner also made an excellent jasper. There were imitators, too, whose work was much poorer in quality, and who did not scruple to use questionable methods of marketing their wares. 'Wedgwood & Co.' appears on pottery made at Ferrybridge, in Yorkshire, by a pottery connected with Ralph Wedgwood, another member of the family, but 'Wedgewood,' with an intrusive 'e,' is the mark of William Smith & Co. of Stockton-on-Tees, against whom Wedgwood obtained an injunction precluding them from using the name, or any deceptive variation of it.

Continental copies, too, are numerous, although most modern reproductions are unmarked. The influence of Wedgwood on Continental wares can hardly be underestimated. In 1763 the Royal Factory at Meissen was being reorganized after the disruption of the Seven Years' War, and the neo-classical style was becoming popular. Unsuited to porcelain, but in many ways admirably adapted to the new creamware of Wedgwood, neo-classicism ousted *rococo*. An extensive export trade grew up almost overnight, and made serious inroads into markets formerly supplied by Meissen. The *faïence* industry capitulated progressively until, by 1800, only two factories still remained in Delft, and the French factories who survived changed to *faïence-fine* in the English manner. Even factories in Sweden imitated it.

The porcelain factories were as badly affected. Before the end of the century Meissen was copying Wedgwood's jasper under the name of *Wedgwoodarbeit*, and the Royal Factory of Sèvres were using *biscuit* porcelain for the same purpose. Workmen came from the Continent to Staffordshire for the express purpose of purloining Wedgwood's secrets. Louis-Victor Gerverot arrived in England, and took service with Wedgwood in 1786, after having been at Fulda, Ludwigsburg, Frankenthal, Weesp, Schrezheim, and Loosdrecht. In 1795 he accepted the directorship of the Fürstenberg porcelain factory, and it is hardly surprising that the influence of Wedgwood is perceptible in wares made here at the end of the century.

The Duke, Karl Eugen, who owned the Ludwigsburg factory, paid Wedgwood a visit in 1776, and no doubt drew inspiration from it, because, in the same year, the manufacture of creamware was started at Ludwigsburg. Wedgwood's wares were also copied in Thuringia in the 18th century, principally at Ilmenau, where Goethe participated in the running of the factory in his capacity of *Geheimrat* to the Duke, Karl August of Weimar. Portrait medallions, particularly, were made here.

It would be tedious to enumerate all the copies of Wedgwood made in Europe during the 18th century, but the situation was, in fact, a dramatic reversal of that existing in the 17th century, and the first decades of the 18th, when Continental and Far Eastern wares were freely copied in England.

It is, perhaps, permissible for the family, who still operate this world-famous factory, to take even more pride than usual in the achievements of their ancestor, because his success was attained without the aid of subventions from the State or from aristocratic patrons. It was, in fact, one of the few great and successful enterprises of the kind in Europe which was run as a commercial venture. The rise of Staffordshire as one of the most important centers for the production of pottery and porcelain in the modern world was due in no small measure to the work of Josiah Wedgwood.

47. COFFEEPOT. AGATE WARE. STAFFORDSHIRE. C. 1740

Height 26.5 cm. The Syndics of the Fitzwilliam Museum, Cambridge

This extremely fine coffeepot is of solid agate ware. It closely resembles a silver pot of about 1700, and the faceted shape and the nature of the base makes its form more appropriate to the shears and the hammer than to any of the methods of formation in common use by the potter. Although it is here referred to as a coffeepot, it might equally well be a teapot, since some of the early silver teapots were in this form. The effect of wedging together several slabs of differently colored clays is well illustrated by the surface appearance. Somewhat similar pots of silver pattern can be seen in early Derby porcelain, but here the octagonal shape is abandoned in favor of the equally early truncated cone, usually with a conical lid.

48. MUSICIANS. ASTBURY-WHIELDON WARE
STAFFORDSHIRE. C. 1740

Average height, 15 cm. Brighton Art Gallery and Museum (Willett Collection), Brighton, Sussex

The musicians play various instruments, the horn probably being the *cor de chasse*. The early Astbury figures were decorated with differently colored clays under a clear glaze, but this technique gradually gave place to the use of colored glazes in the Whieldon style. Those figures which partake of both the Astbury and the Whieldon techniques, as in the present case, are referred to as 'Astbury-Whieldon.' Musicians of all kinds were frequently depicted in this class of ware, some of which are Negroes. Specimens are now extremely rare.

49. EQUESTRIAN GROUP. WHIELDON WARE
STAFFORDSHIRE. C. 1745

21 cm. Brighton Art Gallery and Museum (Willett Collection), Brighton, Sussex

This group of a girl riding pillion is, in its own way, as distinguished in modeling as anything to come from Staffordshire at the time. It is distinctly English in feeling, and has no ascertainable Continental affiliations. Such models are now extremely rare.

50. DRAGOONS. WHIELDON WARE. STAFFORDSHIRE. C. 1745

26 cm. Brighton Art Gallery and Museum (Willett Collection), Brighton, Sussex

The dragoons are mounted on stallions. The body is light in weight and cream-colored, and the figures are covered with colored glazes. The monogram G R appears on the pistol holsters. These figures are sometimes called hussars, but this type of light cavalry was not established until the beginning of the 19th century. From the muskets which they carry in the right hand they are obviously dragoons, who were cavalrymen trained to fight on foot. They received their name from the fact that the muzzles of their muskets were sometimes ornamented with a dragon's head.

47

48

49

53

54

55

51. SALAD BOWL. WHIELDON WARE. STAFFORDSHIRE. C. 1755

24.2 cm. The Syndics of the Fitzwilliam Museum, Cambridge

This remarkably fine molded bowl is an example of Whieldon's best work. In style it suggests an affinity with some of the ware attributed to Whieldon's association with Josiah Wedgwood, which was made about this time or slightly later. The colored glazes are typical of those referred to as 'tortoiseshell,' and have been exceptionally well-controled. The *rococo* moldings are reminiscent of contemporary silver which no doubt inspired this bowl.

52. HUDIBRAS. RALPH WOOD. STAFFORDSHIRE. C. 1765

Height 30 cm. The Victoria and Albert Museum (Gift: W. Sanders Fiske, Esq.), London

This figure of Hudibras mounted on an ancient nag is one of the finest things in English ceramics. Both the character and artistry of this model are remarkable and impressive. The modeler is reputed to have been Aaron Wood. *Hudibras* was written by Samuel Butler as a satire on the Puritans, and was published in three parts in 1663, 1664, and 1668. The original Hudibras is thought to have been Sir Samuel Luke, a Puritan justice of the peace, and the poem especially amused Charles II. The following quotation aptly refers to the illustration:

'The trenchant blade, Toledo trusty,
For want of fighting was grown rusty,
And eat into itself, for lack
Of some body to hew and hack.'

A standing figure in an otherwise similar pose represents the Dutch Admiral, van Tromp, drawing his sword.

53. THE 'PORTLAND' VASE. JASPER WARE. WEDGWOOD. 1786–1790

25 cm. Collection: Sir John Wedgwood, Leith Hill Place, Surrey

The original 'Portland' or 'Barberini' vase is of cameo glass. It is reputed to have contained the ashes of Alexander Severus, and was probably made in Alexandria about 50 B.C. Its later history is obscure, but in the middle of the 17th century it was in the possession of the Barberini family. The vase was acquired by Sir William Hamilton, English Ambassador to Naples, in 1770, and it was sold by him to the Duchess of Portland. It is now in the British Museum. In 1786 this vase was lent by the Duke of Portland to Josiah Wedgwood to copy in jasper ware. The work was completed in 1790, and pronounced accurate in every detail by Sir Joshua Reynolds, President of the Royal Academy. About 29 copies appear to have been made at this time, although slightly different figures are sometimes quoted. The whereabouts of 16 of this edition are known. There have been several subsequent editions, all small in number, and all of which differ in one way or another from the original version.

54. VASE. JASPER WARE. WEDGWOOD. 1786

46.5 cm. The British Museum, London

The subject of this vase was called, by Wedgwood, the *Apotheosis of Homer*. More correctly it is the crowning of a kitharist. The knop to the cover is in the form of Pegasus on a cloud, and there are Gorgon masks under the handles. The relief work is by Flaxman. On June 14th, 1786, Wedgwood wrote to Sir William Hamilton:

'I lamented much that I could not obtain liberty of the merchant to send the vase, the finest and most perfect I have ever made, and which I have since presented to the British Museum. I enclose a rough sketch of it. It is 18 inches high, and the price is 20 guineas. Mr. Chas. Greville saw it, and wished it was in His Majesty's cabinet at Naples.'

55. VASE. JASPER WARE. WEDGWOOD. LATE 18TH CENTURY

32.5 cm. The Victoria and Albert Museum, London

This vase is in the lilac jasper ware. The color was very rarely used during the 18th century, and was discontinued thereafter. It was difficult to attain, and specimens are inclined to vary in shade. Its use has recently been revived (1960). The vase is decorated with figures of the gods in white relief, with musical trophies at the neck.

56. TEAPOT. ASTBURY WARE. STAFFORDSHIRE. C. 1740

15.5 cm. The Victoria and Albert Museum (Schreiber Collection), London

This teapot has a brown glaze over a red body. The reliefs were stamped out of a cream body and applied under the glaze. They represent the Lion and the Unicorn, the supporters of the Royal Arms, and the central medallion is inscribed, *Honi soit qui mal y pense* (Evil to him who thinks evil). This is an excellent example of a rare group of ware.

57. BEAR JUG. COLORED EARTHENWARE STAFFORDSHIRE. C. 1745

33 cm. The Brighton Art Gallery and Museum (The Willett Collection), Brighton, Sussex

This jug, in the form of a bear clasping a dog between its paws, illustrates the sport of bear-baiting. The head is detachable, and forms a cup. The material is dark in color, and the flat strap handle is grooved on either side, with a formal leaf *motif* as a thumb grip. Coloring is green and manganese, with a yellow collar and muzzle. The same subject is also to be seen in white salt-glazed ware, and in Nottingham brown stoneware. Bearbaiting was a popular sport during the 18th century, and survived in the Midlands until 1835. Catherine Dudley of Stoke Lane, in Staffordshire, kept a bear for hire for this purpose until 1830. Bullbaiting, almost equally popular, also appears both in pottery and porcelain at a somewhat later date.

58. ARBOR GROUP. WHIELDON WARE. STAFFORDSHIRE. C. 1745

18 cm. The Brighton Art Gallery and Museum (Willett Collection), Brighton, Sussex

Lovers in an arbor, colored with green, brownish-yellow, manganese, and gray glazes. The top and back of the arbor are both decorated under the glaze with impressed diaper patterns similar to those to be seen on some salt-glazed service ware. The figures and the applied decoration were modeled by hand. Such groups are exceedingly rare.

59. THE DUKE OF CUMBERLAND. WHIELDON WARE. C. 1750

18 cm. The Brighton Art Gallery and Museum (Willett Collection), Brighton, Sussex

This remarkable portrait bust of William Augustus, Duke of Cumberland and victor of Culloden, is better known from a similar bust in Chelsea porcelain of the raised anchor period. It is probable that Cumberland was the patron of the latter factory. The example shown has a gray wig, the dress is brown, and the face is covered with a transparent glaze over a cream body. The eyes and cheeks are touched with manganese. The socle is colored with gray and manganese glazes.

60. MAN SEATED ON A BUFFALO. WHIELDON WARE STAFFORDSHIRE. C. 1750

17 cm. The Victoria and Albert Museum (Schreiber Collection), London

Molded from a Chinese original and decorated in 'tortoise-shell' glazes, the figure being black. These black-glazed figures are very rare, but are analogous to the black glaze used on service ware which is sometimes misattributed to Jackfield. The point is discussed on page 74.

61. CREAMER. WHIELDON WARE. STAFFORDSHIRE. C. 1750

16.5 cm. The Victoria and Albert Museum (Arthur Hurst Bequest), London

This covered creamer or milk jug is decorated with gray, brown, green, and yellow glazes intermingled. The color is predominantly brown, and it has molded floral and foliate decoration in addition. It is typical of the so-called 'tortoise-shell' glazes associated with Thomas Whieldon at mid-century. The body is a light colored earthenware.

62. TEAPOT. WHIELDON WARE. STAFFORDSHIRE. C. 1755

15.5 cm. The Victoria and Albert Museum (Arthur James Collection), London

This teapot is evidence of the degree of skill in handling their material attained by the potters of Staffordshire soon after mid-century. It has double walls, the outer being pierced with floral patterns. The inner wall is glazed with light brown; the outer is colored with green, yellow, and gray glazes. The technique is remotely derived from late Ming porcelain and stoneware decorated in this way, and it was called in China 'devil's work' – an allusion to the almost superhuman skill thought to be required.

56

58

59

61

62

63

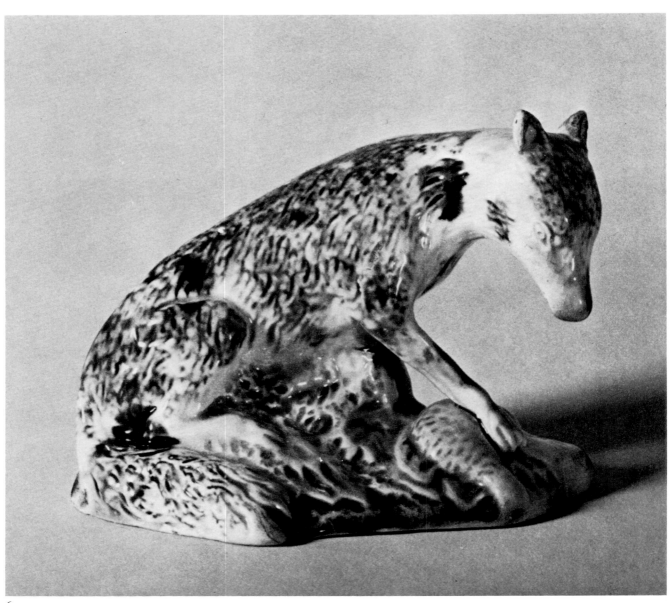

65

66 67

68   69

70

71

72

73 74

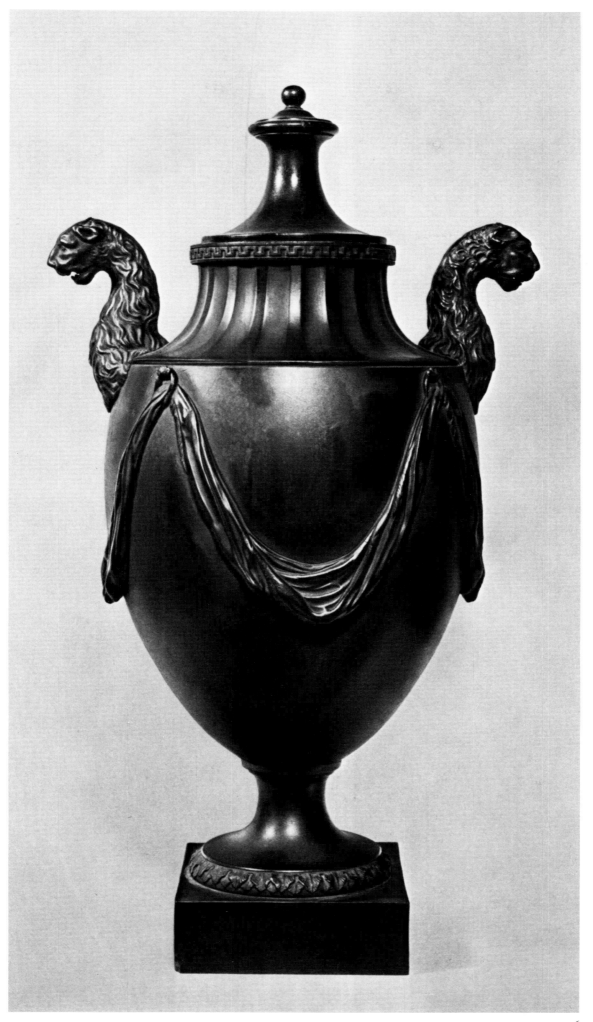

77

79 80

83

63. TOBY JUG. WHIELDON WARE. STAFFORDSHIRE. C. 1760

25 cm. The Brighton Art Gallery and Museum (Willett Collection), Brighton, Sussex

This jug, called the 'Thin Man,' is characteristic of the whole group discussed on page 77. It is typically English in form, and is related to the medieval neck of a pitcher shown in Plate 8. This specimen is decorated with colored glazes, green and manganese, the face and hands being covered with a clear glaze over a buff earthenware body.

---

64. HUNTSMAN. WHIELDON WARE. STAFFORDSHIRE. C. 1760

20.5 cm. The Victoria and Albert Museum (Wallace Elliot Bequest), London

A huntsman and his dog decorated in green, brown, and gray intermingled glazes over a cream-colored earthenware body. The modeling is naive and amusing. The base is somewhat similar to that of the dragoons illustrated on Plate 50, but its sketchy finish suggests a considerable lapse of time between the two models.

---

65. FOX. WHIELDON WARE. STAFFORDSHIRE. C. 1765

9 cm. The Syndics of the Fitzwilliam Museum, Cambridge

This well-observed model of a seated fox is decorated in green, blue, manganese, and yellow glazes in a technique which suggests a late Whieldon origin rather than Ralph Wood. The fur is indicated by incised lines.

---

66. THE VICAR AND MOSES. RALPH WOOD
STAFFORDSHIRE. C. 1770

25 cm. The Brighton Art Gallery and Museum (Willett Collection), Brighton, Sussex

The body is creamware. The decoration is carried out in colored glazes. The woodwork is manganese brown, Moses wears a gray coat and has light brown hair, whilst the Vicar is covered with a transparent glaze. The words, 'The Vicar and Moses,' are impressed on the front of the pulpit in bookbinder's type. Moses sanctimoniously drones through the prayers, whilst the Vicar above him has taken refuge in slumber.

---

67. THE LITTLE CHIMNEY SWEEP. RALPH WOOD. C. 1770

27.5 cm. The Victoria and Albert Museum (Gift: W. Sanders Fiske, Esq.), London

The decoration is in colored glazes. The hat is black, the jacket is grayish-brown, the trousers green. The base is green, and the figure wears black shoes. It was modeled by Jean Voyez, after a model by Cyfflé at Lunéville.

68. THE ROMAN CHARITY. RALPH WOOD
STAFFORDSHIRE. C. 1770

19 cm. The Victoria and Albert Museum (Gift: W. Sanders Fiske, Esq.), London

A woman with two children offering a cup of water to an old man. The subject was popular in Staffordshire during the 18th century, and an impressive group after the painting by Rubens was modeled at Chelsea by Joseph Willems. This group shows considerable differences, and is decorated in green, yellow, gray, and blue glazes on a gray base. The words 'Roman Charity' are impressed.

69. OLD AGE. RALPH WOOD. STAFFORDSHIRE. C. 1770

23 cm. The Victoria and Albert Museum (Gift: W. Sanders Fiske, Esq.), London

He wears a black hat, gray coat, yellow waistcoat, green breeches, and black shoes. The figure is slip cast in a light-colored earthenware body covered with colored glazes. It is in the typical Ralph Wood style.

70. THE DRUNKEN PARSON. RALPH WOOD JR.
STAFFORDSHIRE. C. 1785

26 cm. The Brighton Art Gallery and Museum (Willett Collection), Brighton, Sussex

The group is sometimes called *The Vicar and Moses*, but the name is better reserved for that shown on Plate 66 which is so titled by the factory. The parson wears a black coat and breeches, and his waistcoat is marked with black chevrons. Moses wears a puce surcoat, whilst the base is washed with green and brown, the scrolls being picked out in blue and puce. Moses carries a lantern and supports the vicar on his erratic journey home through the ill-lit streets.

71. JUG. RALPH WOOD. STAFFORDSHIRE. C. 1788

20 cm. The Brighton Art Gallery and Museum (Willett Collection), Brighton, Sussex

This is an example of the well-known 'Fair Hebe' series of jugs which are so-called from the words appearing on the placard above the two figures. Some of these are signed by Voyez and dated 1788. The jug illustrated is slip cast in a light colored earthenware body, and decorated with colored glazes – green, blue, and manganese predominating. The youth is offering a nest full of eggs to his companion.

72. ELOQUENCE. ENOCH WOOD. STAFFORDSHIRE. C. 1790

46.5 cm. The Victoria and Albert Museum (Schreiber Collection), London

The figure wears a purple cloak with a yellow lining. The collar is light brown with dark brown pseudo-embroidery over it. The column is the color of stone, and the base is black.

Eloquence is sometimes called *St. Paul preaching to the Athenians*, but the former is the more likely. On the front of the pedestal is a relief depicting Hermes, the messenger of the gods, flying through clouds, whilst below, Demosthenes orates to the waves. The model may be after a statue by the sculptor, Sir Henry Cheere.

73. MOTHER AND CHILD. ENOCH WOOD. STAFFORDSHIRE. C. 1790

24.5 cm. The Victoria and Albert Museum, London

This group is taken from an existing *terracotta* in the British Museum. The modeling is better than most figures from this source, and is comparable with that illustrated on Plate 72. The flesh is naturally colored, and the woman wears a puce robe with yellow sleeves. The white skirt is dotted with green, whilst the somewhat formal flowers are in polychrome. She is seated on a stool with orange-red legs. The upholstery is black with a yellow fringe. The base is marbled in black and white.

74. ENOCH WOOD. STAFFORDSHIRE. 1821

Life-size. The British Museum, London

This bust is a self-portrait, and was done in 1821 when Enoch Wood was 62 years of age. It is one of the few portraits existing of an 18th century potter, and it testifies to his own skill as a modeler. The bust is of considerable documentary interest. On the reverse is a long incised inscription recording details of the Wood family. For instance, across the shoulders may be read: 'My father Aaron Wood died May 12th 1785 Aged 68 buried at Burslem... He made moulds for all the Potters during the time saltglaze was in general use. April 28th 1821.' An amusing addition protests at the great increase in taxation, and records an amount of £360 as having been paid by Enoch Wood & Co. There are few today who will not sympathize.

75. VASE. WEDGWOOD'S BASALTES WARE. 1769

25.5 cm. Collection: Sir John Wedgwood, Leith Hill Place, Surrey

This vase in black ware is decorated with so-called 'encaustic' painting in iron-red in imitation of Greek red-figure vases. The details are in black, and the inscription at the bottom reads:

Artes Etruriae renascuntur (The art of Etruria is reborn)

On the reverse is the date

June XIII M.DCC.LXIX

and the inscription:

One of the first Day's Productions
at
Etruria in Staffordshire
by
Wedgwood and Bentley

76. VASE. BASALTES WARE. WEDGWOOD & BENTLEY. C. 1770

44.5 cm. Collection: Sir John Wedgwood, Leith Hill Place, Surrey

This vase is an early example, and is of the finest quality. The border ornament at the top is a Greek key fret, whilst the bottom is molded with acanthus leaves. The lion's head handles are crisply modeled and obviously based on metal work. The modeling of the pendant swags, too, leaves nothing to be desired. This vase bears the impressed circular mark of Wedgwood & Bentley on the base.

---

77. EWER. WEDGWOOD & BENTLEY. C. 1770

30.5 cm. Collection: Sir John Wedgwood, Leith Hill Place, Surrey

This ewer, based on a classical model, has a handle in the form of a biting snake, and the grotesque masks under the lip and handle have the remains of oil gilding. The glaze imitates porphyry, and it is a remarkable technical achievement without entirely conforming to the accepted canons of excellence in the ceramic art. It is an example of the neo-classical style which was being popularized at the time by the brothers, Adam.

---

78. PORTRAIT MEDALLIONS. WEDGWOOD'S JASPER WARE
LAST QUARTER OF THE 18TH CENTURY

Collection: Sir John Wedgwood, Leith Hill Place, Surrey

Top: Admiral Hood. Medium-blue jasper ground, gilt metal frame. 9 cm.
Middle: George III and Queen Charlotte. Pale blue jasper ground, gilt metal frames. 8.5 cm.
Bottom: Marie-Antoinette of France. Dark blue jasper ground, dark metal frame. 7 cm.

These are typical of the portrait medallions which were so popular during the 18th century. Similar work was done in basaltes ware, and even, very occasionally, in creamware and caneware.

---

79. MARC ANTONY. WEDGWOOD'S JASPER WARE
LATE 18TH CENTURY

17 cm. The Victoria and Albert Museum (Schreiber Collection), London

The figure wears a tunic with lion-mask pauldrons, and was at one time said to be symbolic of Terror. It is of white jasper on a black socle, and is a remarkable piece of expressive modeling.

80. VOLTAIRE. WEDGWOOD'S CANE-WARE. C. 1777

32 cm. The British Museum, London

This model was first made in 1777 in basaltes ware, and most surviving examples are in this material. Some, with a companion figure of Rousseau, were made in cane-ware, but despite its superiority, this material was apt to discolour during firing. Jean François Marie Arouet de Voltaire was notoriously coy in posing for his portrait. Previously two busts had been done at Sèvres, the first by an ivory carver, Dupont Rosset, and the second by Jacques Caffiéri. Voltaire spent three years in England from 1726, when he became the friend of Bolingbroke.

81. TEAPOT. WEDGWOOD'S CREAMWARE. C. 1760

12 cm. Collection: Sir John Wedgwood, Leith Hill Place, Surrey

This creamware teapot is one of the earliest examples of the use of this material, later to become so popular throughout Europe. The bottom is molded with a basket weave, and there is an open trellis pattern above. The molded fruit and leaves are decorated with green, gray, manganese, and brown glazes as a result of Wedgwood's connection with Whieldon. There is *rococo* molding on the spout, and this is repeated on the cover. The glaze is minutely crazed as a result of a slight disagreement in the contraction rates of body and glaze during cooling.

82. PLATE. WEDGWOOD'S CREAMWARE. C. 1773

24.5 cm. Collection: Sir John Wedgwood, Leith Hill Place, Surrey

This plate decorated with an English view is from the service made for Catherine the Great of Russia, discussed on page 69. The green frog denotes that it was made for the Palace of La Grenouillière in the Tsarkoe Selo.

83. TUREEN. WEDGWOOD'S CREAMWARE. C. 1780

Height 24.5 cm. Length 37 cm. The Victoria and Albert Museum
(Gift: Commander J. A. L. Drummond, from the Lily Antrobus Collection), London

This molded tureen of lobed form has twisted handles, and the knop is in the form of a fruit. The ladle accompanying it is of a silver pattern. In quality it is fully equal to the work of the porcelain factories of the period. The form has some *rococo* elements. The universal popularity of the new material is understandable when the quality of this specimen is taken into account.

SECOND PART: PORCELAIN

CHELSEA (WEST LONDON)

THE ENGLISH MANUFACTURERS of porcelain did not enjoy the advantages of their Continental counterparts. The House of Hanover did not take the same interest in it as Augustus the Strong of Saxony, neither was there a Mme de Pompadour to promote its development. The only English King to have a collection was, in fact, William of Orange, who brought some Japanese porcelain decorated in the style of Sakaida Kakiemon from Holland. This was kept at Hampton Court.

The ships of the East India Company, however, brought much Chinese porcelain, and the Meissen factory of Augustus exported a good deal to England, where its products have always been in demand.

For these reasons porcelain came somewhat late to England. The first reliable record is dated 1742, when Thomas Briand, a Huguenot, demonstrated porcelain of his own manufacture to the Royal Society. It is reasonable to suppose that his formula was not the result of original research, but was based on that already in use at St. Cloud and at Mennecy. In fact, the first porcelain to be made in England very much resembles that of the French factories mentioned.

Since Briand was obviously of French extraction, it seems not unfair to connect his formula with the establishment of a porcelain factory at Chelsea about 1743. The founders were a jeweler, Charles Gouyn, and a silversmith, Nicholas Sprimont, and Sprimont later admitted that he derived his knowledge from a 'casual acquaintance with a chemist who had some knowledge that way.' Briand was both a chemist and a silversmith.

The Chelsea factory was almost immediately successful, and we find that, in 1745, when Charles Adam petitioned the King of France on behalf of the factory at Vincennes, he referred to 'a new factory which has just been established in England for the manufacture of porcelain more beautiful than that of Saxony owing to the nature of its composition.'

Briand, however, did not continue his connection with Chelsea, and about 1745 he was in Derby in company with a certain James Marchand – a circumstance which is discussed on another page.

The porcelain made between the opening of the Chelsea factory and 1750 was often marked with a triangle incised into the base before firing, and a few specimens (e.g. Plate 84) have the word 'Chelsea,' and the year, 1745, in addition. All such wares are commonly referred to as belonging to the 'triangle period,' whether they are marked or not.

The partnership existing between Sprimont and Gouyn came to an end in 1749. In 1750 Sprimont added to an advertisement:

'The Quality and Gentry may be assured that I am not in any shape whatsoever concerned with the goods exposed to sale in St. James's Street, called the Chelsea China Warehouse.'

The proprietor of this warehouse, a certain S. Stables, was probably an agent for Gouyn, and he announced in 1751:

'Seeing it frequently advertised that the proprietor of Chelsea Porcelaine is not concerned in any shape whatsoever in the Goods exposed to Sale in St. James's Street called the Chelsea China Warehouse, in common justice to N. Sprimont (who signed the advertisement) as well as myself, I think it incumbent publicly to declare to the Nobility, Gentry, &c. that my China warehouse is not supplied by any other person than Mr. Charles Gouyn, late Proprietor and Chief Manager of the Chelsea House, who continues to supply me with the most curious goods of that Manufacture, as well useful as ornamental, and which I dispose of at very reasonable rates.'

It can be seen from this that 'China' had become synonymous with porcelain, and the more accurate term 'China ware' was already falling into disuse. These advertisements make it fairly obvious that we have to look for the products of more than one Chelsea factory, and the only possible candidate so far to come to light is a class usually referred to as 'Girl in a Swing' porcelain, from a model in the Victoria and Albert Museum in London, and another similar in the Boston Museum of Fine Arts. This class is here represented by Plate 102.

In course of examination by chemical analysis of examples of Chelsea procelain it was noticed that these specimens contained a much higher quantity of lead oxide than any attributable to the Sprimont factory, and, from an examination of the scanty records, there seems little doubt that the 'Girl in a Swing' and related specimens actually formed part of the stock of S. Stables. So far, no service ware has been identified, and figures are extremely rare.

The break between Sprimont and Gouyn was otherwise marked by the abandonment about 1749 of the kind of porcelain used to manufacture the 'triangle' wares, and the adoption of a new mark – that of an anchor raised on a small oval tablet. The new body was almost equally glassy in appearance, but specimens of comparable size are usually heavier, and instead of tiny specks of greater translucency (the so-called 'pinholes') to be seen when 'triangle' porcelain is held up to the light, bright patches about one-third of an inch across (referred to as 'moons') are often present in plates and similar flat ware. These 'moons' can also be observed in some early French porcelain, and in a few early specimens from Meissen.

Patronage for Sprimont's factory from a quarter near to the throne is probable. A workman named Mason, who was at Chelsea, had this to say in his later years:

'It was first carried on by the Duke of Cumberland (William Augustus, second son of George II and victor of Culloden) and Sir Everard Fawkener, and the sole management was intrusted to a foreigner named Sprimont. I think Sir Everard died about 1755 (actually, in 1758) when Mr. Sprimont became sole proprietor.'

In 1751 Sir Charles Hanbury Williams, Ambassador to the Saxon Court, wrote to Henry Fox, the Baron Holland, who was then Secretary-at-War:

'I received a letter about ten days ago from Sir Everard Fawkener who is, I believe, concerned in the manufacture of China at Chelsea. He desired me to send over models for different pieces from hence in order to furnish the undertakers with good designs, and would have me send over fifty or three score pounds worth. But I thought it better and cheaper for the manufacturers to give them leave to take any of my China from Holland House, and to copy what they like.' Direct proof of Cumberland's intervention is still wanting, but Sir Everard Fawkener was his secretary, and the style of the factory's work changed considerably during the year of Fawkener's death in 1758.

About 1754 Nicholas Sprimont was the author of a document asking for discriminatory taxes against imports of Meissen porcelain. This was entitled, *The Case of the Undertaker of the Chelsea Manufacture of Porcelain ware*, and begins:

'This undertaker, a silversmith by profession, from a casual acquaintance with a chemist who had some knowledge that way, was tempted to make a trial, which, upon the progress he made, he was encouraged to pursue with great labour and expense... The manufacture was thus put upon a more extensive footing.'

In 1753 Chelsea appears to have made alterations in the porcelain body used, and production was in greater quantity than hitherto. About the same time we find that figures by Kändler and Eberlein at Meissen became popular as a source of inspiration, and some Chelsea figures are little more than superb copies. The new period was marked by the adoption of a painted anchor in red as a mark, and this is usually quite small, and often added in an inconspicuous position. From about this time onwards we find that most specimens contain a quantity of bone ash – an addition to the porcelain body adopted at Bow some years before which is later discussed in greater detail.

We have two valuable contemporary sources of information about the wares being manufactured at this time in the form of auction sale catalogues for 1755 and 1756, and many of the lots can convincingly be identified with surviving examples.

Sprimont fell ill in 1756, and some of the painters went to Bow, in the east end of London. This, no doubt, accounts for such rarities as the Bow plate pictured on Plate 119 which has been superbly painted by a well-known Chelsea hand, and which serves equally well as an illustration of Chelsea porcelain thus decorated. Little work seems to have been done until 1758. Fawkener died in this year, and Cumberland's patronage was probably withdrawn, if Mason is a reliable witness. Perhaps connected with this circumstance was the change in style from that of the German factory of Meissen, which Cumberland (as a member of the House of Hanover) may have preferred, to the French styles of Sèvres, which were probably nearer to Sprimont's own taste.

The beginning of this period is marked by the adoption of a new glaze, which is soft and fusible and much more like that to be seen on early Sèvres porcelain, as well as such Sèvres ground colors as the *gros bleu*, and the *rose Pompadour* (see Plate 93), known in England as 'claret,' and sometimes, quite erroneously, as *rose du Barry*. This change was marked by the adoption of an anchor in gold as a mark. In England particularly, where Meissen porcelain has usually been preferred to that of Sèvres, it is hardly surprising to find that the red anchor wares are the more highly esteemed.

In 1763 Sprimont again fell ill, and this time he advertised the factory for sale. It is evident that very little work was done between this year and 1769, when the factory was first purchased by James Cox, and then resold to William Duesbury of Derby in February, 1770. For some years Duesbury ran the two factories in combination, and the work of this period is often referred to as 'Chelsea Derby' where there is reason to assume manufacture at the former Chelsea factory. For the most part differentiation is not particularly easy, unless the mark sometimes used has been added. Sprimont died in 1771.

The wares of the 'triangle' period are, for the most part, based on contemporary silver forms, and the examples illustrated on Plates 84 and 99 are both of this nature. Dated specimens are very rare, but a number exist. Enamel decoration occurs occasionally, and the palette is distinctive. Most surviving examples are undecorated.

The early raised anchor wares often imitate the *blanc de Chine* of Tê Hua, particularly in the use of raised sprigs of prunus blossom. This was also done during the 'triangle' period, when the flowers of the tea plant were sometimes used in addition. Octagonal and fluted shapes were derived from the Japanese porcelain of Arita, and decoration is often in the style of Kakiemon. Much rarer are specimens decorated with Fable subjects, and these are to be seen on plates of silver form (Plate 87). Rare indeed are things painted with harbor scenes and landscapes in the manner of Meissen, some of which are by William Duvivier.

The Fables are usually based on an edition of Aesop published in 1687, with drawings by Francis Barlow, the Fables rendered into English verse by Mrs. Aphra Behn, the novelist and dramatist who died in 1689. Some of the most amusing were painted by Jeffryes Hamett O'Neale, an Irish miniature painter, whose work is, perhaps, more often seen on Worcester porcelain.

At a slightly later date, about 1754, we find painted decoration of botanical specimens, probably inspired by the Meissen *deutsche Blumen*, which were based on illustrations by Philip Miller of plants in the Chelsea Physic Gardens of Sir Hans Sloane, President of the Royal Society, who gave his name to Sloane Square in Chelsea. Miller's *Gardeners' Dictionary* of 1735 contained 300 engravings after 'Drawings taken from Nature,' and in another work he discusses such things as the culture of the pineapple. That this exotic tropical fruit could be grown in hothouses accounts for its appearance in the form of porcelain tureens and other things.

The *rococo* fashion for plates in the form of leaves, and tureens in the form of fruits, vegetables, animals such as the rabbit, and birds, was particularly popular at Chelsea. The reader is referred to the superb tureens in the form of birds shown on Plates 89 and 90 which far surpass anything else of the kind made in Europe at the time.

The change to wares of the gold anchor type is first apparent in 1756, when both rich gilding and the *gros bleu* ground are mentioned in the sale catalogue for that year. The latter ground, curiously enough, is called, for no ascertainable reason, 'Mazarin' blue. 'A bason and ewer of a fine mazareen blue enamell'd in birds and richly chas'd and gilt.' An example of this kind, which is a little later, can be seen on Plate 97.

In 1763 Queen Charlotte ordered a service for her brother, the Duke of Mecklenburg-Strelitz, and, at the same time, a duplicate service differing only in the form of the curves over the small *gros bleu* panels (convex in the original service, concave in the duplicate) was made, and reputedly sold for £1.150, perhaps equivalent to about £30.000 or $70.000. in today's currency. A plate from this service appears on Plate 96. Several examples of magnificent bird painting are shown. These *Fantasie-Vögel* of Meissen were called exotic birds in England, and were even more exotic than those which inspired them.

Few figures of the 'triangle' period are known. Some *putti* in the form of candlesticks were made at this time, but generally nothing of importance was attempted until the raised anchor period. At the extreme end of the period, however, we find one or two things like the group of Lovers shown on Plate 101 which is the equal of anything to be done at Meissen or Sèvres. A specimen which is almost equally early, to be seen on Plate 100, is reputed to be a portrait of the actress, Peg Woffington. A pair of sphinxes of the late triangle period with the head of the actress, Kitty Clive, a portrait of whom appears on Plate 128, also exist. These sphinxes, of which a Bow example appears on Plate 129, were derived from the work of the 17th century French designer, Jean Bèrain, who used similar *motifs* quite frequently. Later it became fashionable for Court beauties to have themselves modeled in this form in *terracotta*, and the mode crossed the Channel about 1750 and was taken up by the early porcelain factories.

Belonging to the raised anchor period are some excellent figures of birds, taken from plates illustrating *The Natural History of Birds* by George Edwardes. The latter wrote at the time:

'I have observed that several of our manufacturers that imitate the China ware have filled the shops in London with images modelled after the figures in my *History of Birds*, most of which are sadly represented as to shape and colouring.'

A specimen in this *genre* from the Bow factory can be seen on Plate 117. Despite their popularity at the time, such things are very rare today.

To the same period belongs a figure of a nurse and child after a pottery model by Bartélemy de Blenod at the Avon pottery in France of the early part of the 17th century, which was also repeated at Worcester. By far the most distinguished, however, is a series of figures here represented by Plate 103. In some of these various authorities have traced a resemblance in style to the work of the sculptor, Louis-François Roubiliac. It is worth mention that Sprimont was godfather to Roubiliac's daughter, Sophie, in 1744, and the superb Chelsea head on Plate 85 is thought to be a portrait of this small girl who would then be about six years old. A series of later models marked with an 'R' impressed, however, are certainly not the work of Roubiliac as was once suggested.

Another hand of uncommon skill is represented by the figure shown on Plate 104. Most of these belong to the early red anchor period, and, although they are obviously inspired by Kändler, are superbly modeled in a porcelain body of remarkable excellence. A few rare groups were modeled after plates appearing in the *Délices de l'enfance*, engraved by J.J.Bachelou after François Boucher.

The *hippocampi*, a pair of mythological water horses to be seen on Plate 107, recall the predilection of the *rococo* style for themes connected with water, also to be seen in the early crawfish salts (Plate 98).

The Italian Comedy (*commedia dell' Arte*) is here represented by Pierrot on Plate 108, and Pantaloon and Columbine, based on a model by Kändler, on Plate 88. This improvised play, performed by companies of strolling players, was immensely popular throughout Europe, and its characters were frequently used as a subject for porcelain figures and for decoration.

The gold anchor period is notable for some overlarge figures, of which *Una and the Lion*, about 30 inches in height, is an example. The *rococo* molding of the German factories which, at this time, was beginning to be elevated above the base, particularly in the groups of Bustelli at Nymphenburg and Lück at Frankenthal, was not popular in this form at Chelsea. Instead, an arbor of modeled flowers and leaves was used, and this can be well seen in the group on Plate 95, which is in the full tide of the gold anchor style. This 'bocage,' by which name it was known, was also used at Bow and Derby, but is much more crudely executed at both places.

The later Chelsea figures, usually referred to as Chelsea-Derby, are in the Louis Seize style – transitional between *rococo* and neo-classical – and they are decorated in pale pastel shades, in contrast to the much stronger colors used during the period of Sprimont's proprietorship. *Biscuit*, or unglazed, porcelain – introduced by Bachelier at Sèvres in 1752 – was not used until after Duesbury's purchase of the factory. An example of the kind appears on Plate 113.

84. JUG. CHELSEA PORCELAIN. TRIANGLE PERIOD. 1745

11.5 cm. Collection: Major-General Sir Harold Wernher, Bart., Luton Hoo, Bedfordshire

This small jug has a pure white glassy body with some 'pinholes' when it is viewed by transmitted light. Incised into the base is the word 'Chelsea,' and the date, '1745.' We owe these jugs, perhaps, to Sprimont's early profession of silversmith, since they are undoubtedly a silver shape, and some examples survive in this medium. They were molded, and several molds were used, which accounts for minor differences between various specimens. They appear to have been made over a period of five or six years, and later forgeries, accused by a thicker body and clumsy form, are not uncommon.

---

85. HEAD OF A YOUNG GIRL. CHELSEA PORCELAIN
RAISED ANCHOR PERIOD. C. 1752

19 cm. The Ashmolean Museum of Fine Art (Cyril Andrade Collection), Oxford

This superb head of a girl was discovered in 1937. The distinguished modeling has caused it to be attributed to the hand of the sculptor, Louis-François Roubiliac, and the subject is probably his daughter, Sophie, to whom Sprimont was godfather in August, 1744. The apparent age of the subject and the date of manufacture (1752) agree sufficiently well for this hypothesis to be acceptable. Roubiliac frequently carved figures of children, and several examples of work of the kind are known.

---

86. DISH. CHELSEA PORCELAIN. RAISED ANCHOR PERIOD. C. 1752

20 cm. Collection: W. R. B. Young, Esq., St. Leonards-on-Sea, Sussex

A shape not unusual at the period. The tulips, primroses, and gentians recall the fashion for *deutsche Blumen* at Meissen and the flower painting on contemporary Vincennes porcelain. The palette is distinctive, and, to some extent, resembles that of Vincennes. The chocolate edging to the rim is undoubtedly derived from Japanese porcelain decorated by Kakiemon.

---

87. DISH. CHELSEA PORCELAIN. EARLY RED ANCHOR PERIOD
C. 1753

23 cm. The Victoria and Albert Museum (Schreiber Collection), London

The molded form of this dish is based on contemporary silver in the *rococo* style. The center is superbly painted with the Fable of the Dog, the Cock, and the Fox. The hand is that of Jeffryes Hamett O'Neale, and it is interesting to compare this with the much later Fable of the Bear and the Honey from the same hand on Plate 146. The styles are recognizably the same, and they both have the same humorous touch, but the freedom of drawing is greater in the earlier specimen, and the coloring not so heavy.

The form of the dish should be compared with that illustrated on Plate 91.

84

85

86

87

89

91

92

93

94

95

97

88. PANTALOON AND COLUMBINE. CHELSEA PORCELAIN RED ANCHOR PERIOD. C. 1755

18.5 cm. Collection: Major-General Sir Harold Wernher, Bart., Luton Hoo, Bedfordshire

This superb group of players from the Italian Comedy is derived from a Meissen model by Johann Joachim Kändler. The Comedy was extremely popular throughout Europe at this time, and was performed by groups of strolling players. It is a frequent subject of porcelain figures and decorations, the source quite often being Riccoboni's *Histoire du théâtre italien* of 1730. Pantaloon was a miserly merchant of Venice married to a young and unfaithful wife, whilst Columbine was a coquettish serving maid.

89. GAMECOCKS. CHELSEA PORCELAIN. RED ANCHOR PERIOD C. 1755

Height 23 cm. Length 38 cm. The Syndics of the Fitzwilliam Museum, Cambridge

A large pair of tureens in the form of life-size gamecocks, naturally colored. The handles are modeled as feathers. These superb examples appear to be unique, and are of the finest quality. The sport of cockfighting was probably introduced into England by the Romans, although the first record of it is to be found in the reign of Henry II. During the 18th century a number of cockpits were established in London, notably at Westminster, Drury Lane, Birdcage Walk, Pall Mall, the Haymarket, and Covent Garden, and matches were the subject of large wagers. The sport was made illegal in 1849, but still survives in rural districts, particularly in the North of England.

90. TUREEN. CHELSEA PORCELAIN. RED ANCHOR PERIOD C. 1755

Height 20 cm. Width 44 cm. The Trustees of the Cecil Higgins Museum, Bedford

This remarkable tureen depicting two pigeons on a nest appears in the Chelsea sale catalogue of 1755 as 'a double pigeon big as life.' A tureen in the form of gamecocks appears on Plate 89, whilst the domestic hen and the goose were also made in this form. They are now extremely rare, and were inspired originally by the work of Kändler at Meissen.

91. DISH. CHELSEA PORCELAIN. GOLD ANCHOR PERIOD C. 1760

22 cm. Hastings Museum and Art Gallery, Hastings, Sussex

The form of this dish is based on a silver pattern more often to be seen during the raised anchor period (1750-52). It is an interesting survival. The superb exotic bird painting is typical of the style of the gold anchor period, and the dish bears the appropriate mark. A plate of silver form of the earlier date is shown on Plate 87.

92. GROUP OF CHILDREN. CHELSEA PORCELAIN
GOLD ANCHOR PERIOD. C. 1760

13 cm. Collection: Major-General Sir Harold Wernher, Bart., Luton Hoo, Bedfordshire

This group is an excellent example of the more restrained gold anchor figures which equal those of the red anchor period in quality. It can, perhaps, be regarded as transitional. The dresses are colored in Chelsea versions of the *rose Pompadour* of Sèvres, referred to at the time as 'claret.' The moldings of the *rococo* base are comparatively simple.

93. INKSTAND. CHELSEA PORCELAIN. GOLD ANCHOR PERIOD
C. 1760

Width 21.5 cm. Collection: Major-General Sir Harold Wernher, Bart., Luton Hoo, Bedfordshire

This inkstand comprises an inkwell, pounce pot, taper stick, and pen tray which has a lamb as a handle to the cover. The ground color is the Chelsea version of the *rose Pompadour* of Sèvres. This was called 'claret' at the time, and later received the gross misnomer of *rose du Barry*. The color was, of course, devised at Sèvres in 1757 and discontinued about 1764, the year of the death of Madame de Pompadour. It was not used thereafter, except on forgeries. No connection with the du Barry, therefore, is possible. The exotic bird painting on this inkstand leans heavily on the work of Sèvres, and the gilding is extremely rich. The Chelsea use of the *rococo* is usually, as in this specimen, restrained and in good taste.

94. VASE. CHELSEA PORCELAIN. GOLD ANCHOR MARK. C. 1760

47 cm. Collection: Major-General Sir Harold Wernher, Bart., Luton Hoo, Bedfordshire

One of a pair of vases, magnificently painted with exotic birds in the manner of Sèvres. The work is fully equal to that of the French Royal factory. The *rococo* scroll handles also have the addition of modeled fruit and flowers painted in natural colors.

95. THE DANCING LESSON. CHELSEA PORCELAIN
GOLD ANCHOR PERIOD. C. 1760

Height 46 cm. Width 33 cm. The London Museum, Kensington Palace

This large and imposing group of a shepherd playing a hurdy-gurdy (a kind of automatic lute) whilst his companion teaches two dogs to dance is in the full tide of the gold anchor style. It appears to have been made as a companion group to the much better known *Music Lesson,* and this is the only version of the subject known to me. Although the flowering may-bush is not, perhaps, an ideal background for the figures, this group has seldom been surpassed anywhere for sheer virtuosity in a difficult material.

96. PLATE. CHELSEA PORCELAIN. GOLD ANCHOR PERIOD. C. 1763

22 cm. Collection: W. R. B. Young, Esq., St. Leonards-on-Sea, Sussex

This plate is similar in decoration to the service given by George III and Queen Charlotte to the Duke of Mecklenburg-Strelitz in 1763. The birds are reputed to have been painted by Zachariah Boreman, later a landscape painter at Derby (Plate 125). The influence of Sèvres is noticeable.

97. PLATE. CHELSEA PORCELAIN. GOLD ANCHOR PERIOD. C. 1763

23 cm. Collection: W. R. B. Young, Esq., St. Leonards-on-Sea, Sussex

The *gros bleu* panels with birds in gilt silhouette show the influence of the decorative styles of Vincennes. The *gros bleu* ground was called, at Chelsea, 'Mazareen blue.' Honey-gilding (i.e. gold ground up in honey and lightly fired) is raised and chased. This is an example of the finest work of the period.

98. SALT. CHELSEA PORCELAIN. TRIANGLE PERIOD. 1745–1750

Height 9 cm. Width 12 cm. Trustees of the Cecil Higgins Museum, Bedford

This salt has the typical glassy body of the period, and the crawfish is colored red-brown, the shells being in yellow, brownish-red, and coral red. The seaweed is touched with green. This has a silver prototype, and is similar in many ways to a silver-gilt salt of 1742 in the Royal Collections at Buckingham Palace which bears the maker's mark of Nicholas Sprimont. In the latter case a crab replaces the crawfish. The subject belongs to an early phase of the *rococo* style, which arrived somewhat late in England and first appears in silver (see Plate 84).

99. COFFEEPOT. CHELSEA PORCELAIN. TRIANGLE PERIOD 1745–1750

20 cm. The Trustees of the Cecil Higgins Museum, Bedford

The molded decoration is derived from Tê Hua (Fukien Province) and probably represents the tea plant, rather than the more usual prunus blossom. The form is a silver pattern, and the body is glassy, with 'pinholes.' The top of the handle is decorated with acanthus molding. This example should be compared with Plate 84, which represents another copy of a silver jug belonging to this group.

147

100. SPHINX. CHELSEA PORCELAIN. RAISED ANCHOR PERIOD
C. 1750

Length 16 cm. Height 10 cm. Trustees of the Cecil Higgins Museum, Bedford

This may be intended as a portrait of Peg Woffington, but the attribution is very uncertain. It approaches more closely to the conventional sphinx of Egypt, and is much less *rococo* in feeling than the Bow example shown on Plate 129. Nevertheless, it is probably intended to be a portrait. The remains of a raised anchor can clearly be seen on the front of the base. This mark was stamped on a small oval pad and applied, but it has often become detached, wholly or in part. The original site of such a mark can be identified from an oval patch, bare of glaze, when this has happened.

101. THE LOVERS. CHELSEA PORCELAIN. C. 1750

22.5 cm. The British Museum, London

This superb group, one of the finest things in English porcelain, belongs to a class of Chelsea marked with a crown and trident in blue which is transitional between the triangle and raised anchor periods, and of which few specimens still exist. Only one other example of the present group is known, in the collection of the late Sigmund Katz in the United States, and this has some slight divergences which arose during the 'repairing' process. The original inspiration appears to have been the work of Vincennes, and reference should be made to Plate 102 which shows a close copy of a Vincennes group.

102. HERCULES AND OMPHALE. CHELSEA PORCELAIN
'GIRL IN A SWING' CLASS. C. 1750

25 cm. The Syndics of the Fitzwilliam Museum, Cambridge

The model appears to have been derived from a similar group made at Vincennes, the origin being an engraving from a painting by Lemoyne. The principal difference between this and the Vincennes version is that the third figure of Eros is missing (see page 125).

103. TOUCH. CHELSEA PORCELAIN. RED ANCHOR PERIOD. C. 1753

27.5 cm. The London Museum, Kensington Palace

This superb group comes from a set of the Senses, and is the one most rarely illustrated. It has been suggested, with some justification, that the original model was from the hand of the sculptor, Louis-François Roubiliac. The woman's hair is delicately colored, with a light puce band, and her robe is decorated with flowers reminiscent of the *indianische Blumen* of Meissen. The falcon is colored puce, whilst the tortoise has a black shell with yellow markings. For another example attributed to Roubiliac, see Plate 85.

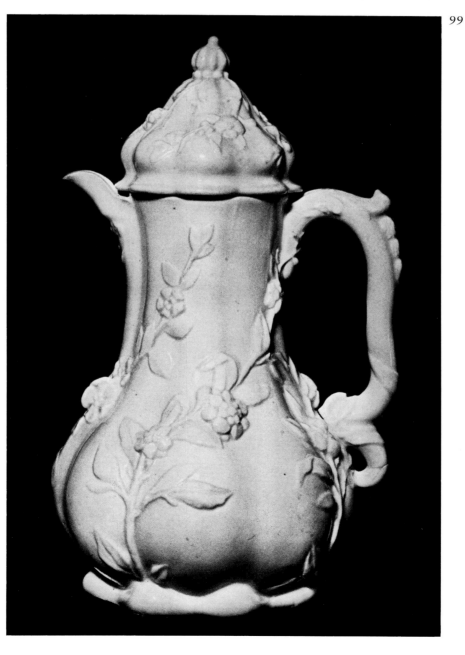

100

101

104

105

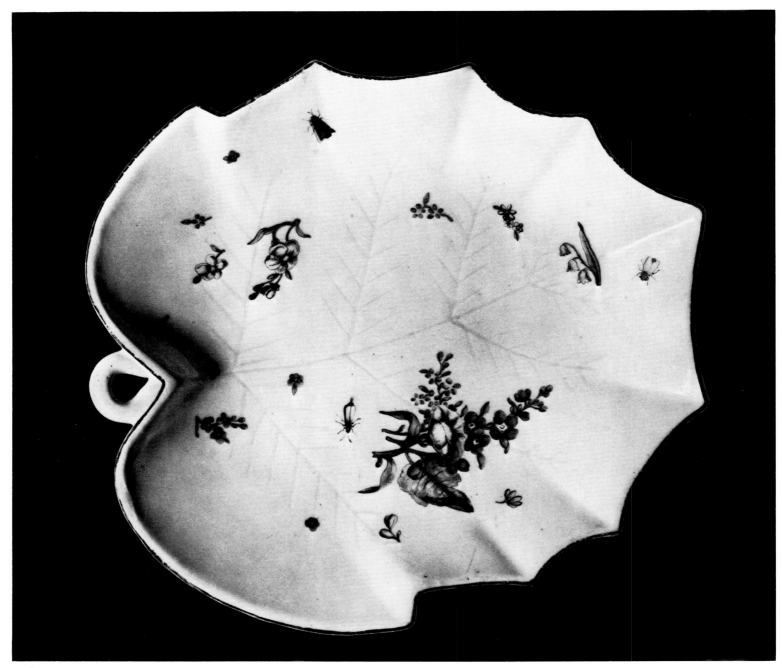

106

109

III

112

104. LABORER. CHELSEA PORCELAIN
EARLY RED ANCHOR PERIOD. C. 1753

20 cm. The Syndics of the Fitzwilliam Museum, Cambridge

The superb modeling of this figure is enhanced by the slightness of the coloring which allows the quality of the porcelain to be seen and appreciated. He wears a black hat and shoes, an effective contrast to the white surface, whilst his breeches are colored a pale yellow. The flowers on the base are conventionally colored, and the base itself is washed with green. This figure represents a small series, all of the finest quality, modeled by an unidentified hand. All of them can be placed to about 1752–1753 with reasonable certainty.

105. TEAPOT. CHELSEA PORCELAIN
EARLY RED ANCHOR PERIOD. C. 1753

14.5 cm. The Trustees of the Cecil Higgins Museum, Bedford

This teapot, decorated with a pattern of Quails derived from Japanese porcelain, is molded with strawberries and leaves in a manner similar to that on the reverse of the dish illustrated on Plate 106. The form is an obvious silver pattern. Japanese porcelain from Arita (Hizen Province) decorated by Sakaida Kakiemon is noted for asymmetricality, and for the careful balance preserved between the pattern and the quality of the white porcelain surface. This quality is well-preserved at Chelsea in wares in this style.

106. LEAF DISH. CHELSEA. RED ANCHOR PERIOD. C. 1753

22 cm. Collection: W.R.B.Young, Esq., St. Leonards-on-Sea, Sussex

The ribs of the leaf are indented, and the polychrome flowers – convolvulus, forget-me-nots, and lilies of the valley – are painted in sprays. The back of the dish is molded with stalk and tendrils, strawberry leaves and fruit. In this it is related to the teapot shown on Plate 105. By transmitted light the body shows a large number of 'moons.'

107. HIPPOCAMPI. CHELSEA PORCELAIN
RED ANCHOR PERIOD. C. 1754

Height 15 cm. Length 29 cm. The Trustees of the Cecil Higgins Museum, Bedford

One has a *putto* as a rider. He is touched with flesh color. The hippocampi have tails painted slightly with puce, and washed with a faint grayish-green enamel over incised scales. The reins are light brown. These are obviously part of a table decoration on a much larger scale. The *rococo* theme of water is once again in evidence, and the same fabulous animals appear at Meissen, in particular with a figure of Neptune modeled by Kändler about 1745.

108. PIERROT. CHELSEA PORCELAIN. RED ANCHOR PERIOD
C. 1754

15 cm. The Trustees of the Cecil Higgins Museum, Bedford

This figure is of Pierrot, or Pedrolino, a character in the Italian Comedy. He was usually a valet in love with a serving maid, but the character later assumed greater importance. Pagliacco is a later form who provided the Prologue to performances – Mascagni's opera, *I Pagliacci*, for instance. The hat and suit are pale mauve, the shoes are orange-red, and the straps holding the drum are yellow. The applied flowers are conventionally colored. The model owes much to Meissen. The extension of the foot beyond the base greatly improves the composition at the expense of making it more vulnerable.

---

109. WOMAN IN A CRINOLINE. CHELSEA PORCELAIN
RED ANCHOR PERIOD. C. 1755

15.5 cm. The Trustees of the Cecil Higgins Museum, Bedford

This figure is, by general consent, one of the finest to come from the Chelsea factory. The modeling has been executed with rare skill, and the pose and general composition could hardly be bettered. Her gown is white, with a puce lining, and it is decorated with gold flower sprigs. The underskirt is an egg-yolk yellow, a little paler than the Meissen color, and is painted with the so-called India flowers *(indianische Blumen)* derived from this factory. The shoes are puce, and the gown has orange-red bows.

---

110. MAP SELLER. CHELSEA PORCELAIN. RED ANCHOR PERIOD
C. 1755

18.5 cm. The Trustees of the Cecil Higgins Museum, Bedford

This excellent model is remarkable for being an almost exact copy of a Meissen figure by Kändler of about 1745. The coloring is, of course, in the paler Chelsea palette, and the map is different, that of the Meissen example being of part of Germany. The figure was also copied at Derby in England, and elsewhere in Germany. It was extremely popular at the time (cf. Fischer Collection catalogue, No. 790, page 120 and Berling, *Meissner Porzellan*, Plate 90).

---

111. CHAMBER CANDLESTICK. CHELSEA PORCELAIN
RED ANCHOR PERIOD. C. 1755.

16 cm. Collection: Major-General Sir Harold Wernher, Bart., Luton Hoo, Bedfordshire

This has a handle at the back for carrying. Table candlesticks lack this feature. The sconce has green-edged leaves with puce veining. The bird has a black head, and a green lined back. The wings are black, and tipped with blue at the shoulder. The *rococo* scroll base is much finer in quality than from most English factories, and, in fact, approaches those from Nymphenburg. This model can be regarded as transitional between the red and gold anchor styles.

112. GEORGE III. CHELSEA-DERBY PORCELAIN. C. 1773

37 cm. The British Museum, London

This is taken from the central figure in a portrait of the Royal Family by the artist, Johann Zoffany, R. A., who was a fashionable portrait painter of the time. The figure is in *biscuit* porcelain. The base and pedestal have a blue ground decorated with gilt traceries in the manner of Sèvres, whilst the crown rests on a crimson cushion fringed with gold. A somewhat similar scheme was used at Sèvres for a portrait of Louis XV, and this may have suggested the coloring of the illustration. The other members of the Royal Family are represented in two flanking groups modeled at the same time, perhaps by John Bacon. The three groups are mentioned in a catalogue published by Duesbury in June, 1773.

113. GROUP. CHELSEA-DERBY PORCELAIN. C. 1775

22 cm. The Victoria and Albert Museum (Schreiber Collection), London

This group, entitled *Pensent-ils au raisin?*, is based on an engraving by Jacques-Phillipe Le Bas after a painting done in 1747 by François Boucher. The flesh is naturally colored, the dresses are touched with gilding, and the grapes are purple and green. The color scheme is typical of the pastel shades used during the early part of the neo-classical period.

THIS PORCELAIN FACTORY was established in 1744, and it is fair to say that it had its roots in what was then the colony of Virginia. André Duché, a Huguenot settled in Savannah, Georgia, discovered both white china clay and a fusible feldspathic rock in Virginia sometime after 1730. The Governor of the colony, General Oglethorpe, wrote to London in 1738:

'An earth is found which Duché the potter has baked into China ware.'

Duché, however, could not find the necessary financial support for his new project, and in the Spring of 1744 he arrived in London. His first contact seems to have been with a portrait painter and engraver, Thomas Frye, who was associated with Edward Heylyn. The latter owned a glass manufactory at Bow. These two men took out a patent for a porcelain body in 1744, of which the following is an extract:

'The material is an earth, the product of the Cherokee nation in America, called *unaker*.'

Duché seems to have returned home in 1745, and in this year a Quaker apothecary of Plymouth, William Cookworthy, who had been experimenting with the manufacture of porcelain, wrote:

'I have lately had with me the person who has discovered the Chinese earth. He had with him several samples of the China ware which I think were equal to the Asiatic. It was found on the back of Virginia... He has gone for a cargo of it, having bought from the Indians the whole country where it rises. They can import it for £13 per ton, and by that means afford their china as cheap as common stoneware, but they intend only to go about 30 per cent. under the Company.'

The 'Company' in this context is the East India Company which was importing Chinese porcelain in large quantities, and it is interesting to speculate on whether Cookworthy intends to refer to the import from Virginia of white china clay as a raw material, or of the finished product. Certainly Virginian china clay was imported about this time and later, but if we take the former reading, his letter suggests that the East India Company was importing similar clay from China. It would, of course, make excellent ballast for sailing ships, and it is possible that the Chelsea factory made use of white clay from Chinese sources, since Devon china clay had not been discovered.

Nothing survives which can convincingly be identified with the formula patented by Heylyn and Frye in 1744, and in 1749 Frye, alone, took out a fresh patent which specified:

'... a new method of making a certain ware which is not inferior in beauty and fineness and is rather superior in strength than the earthenware which is brought from the East Indies...'

This new body contained calcined bones, usually referred to as bone ash. Hitherto the porcelain made in England had been a mixture of clay and ground glass in the French manner, and, like all artificial porcelains of the kind, it was difficult to fire successfully. This was principally due to the extremely critical firing temperature inevitably attached to such porcelain bodies, and bone ash, whilst detracting somewhat from the ultimate appearance, allowed a much greater temperature latitude, with a consequent lower percentage of wastage. Nevertheless, the finer Bow porcelain rivaled that of Chelsea in quality at times, particularly the specimens to be seen on Plate 117 and Plate 119.

Thomas Frye obtained financial assistance from two London merchants named Weatherby and Crowther, and the Bow factory started to manufacture porcelain on a commercial scale in 1749. The factory was named 'New Canton,' and the earliest documentary specimens are some circular inkwells inscribed 'Made at New Canton,' and dated either 1750 or 1751. These are exceedingly rare.

The early wares were often decorated with raised sprigs of prunus blossom in imitation of the *blanc de Chine* of Tê Hua, in Fukien Province, or painted in colors with patterns derived from the work of Sakaida Kakiemon at the Japanese factory of Arita, the most popular design being of quails. It is, perhaps, questionable whether these patterns were copied directly from Japanese porcelain. It is more probable that they were taken from the work of Continental factories. The quail pattern was certainly used at Meissen, and in particular does it appear on porcelain made at Chantilly, where the earliest decoration was almost exclusively in this style. The Chantilly painters copied Japanese porcelain in the collection of the Prince de Condé. Chinese patterns from the *famille rose* are comparatively common from Bow, and much service ware painted in blue underglaze was made for the cheaper market. Chelsea blue painted wares, on the other hand, are almost nonexistent.

Although Bow did not attempt to appeal to the same aristocratic market as Chelsea, its figures are often extremely fine. Some of the best are by an unknown artist, referred to as the 'Muses Modeller' because his hand was first identified from a series of the nine Muses done about 1750. An example of his work is illustrated on Plate 114 where its characteristics are discussed. He appears to have been French in origin, probably a Huguenot expatriate, and this much may be deduced from an inscription on the base of the Muse, Erato: *Eraton for the love.* The construction of this sentence is certainly not English, but a literal translation from French.

John Bacon, the sculptor and Academician, is said to have worked for the Bow factory. He was first apprenticed to Crispe of Bow Churchyard, 'an eminent maker of porcelain, who taught him (Bacon) the art of modelling various figures and groups' according to one authority. Bacon has been credited with the figures illustrated on Plate 133, but there is no certain evidence for the assumption. He supplied models both to Wedgwood and to Duesbury at Derby, and it is possible that the portrait of George III on Plate 112 is by his hand.

For many reasons the most interesting Bow artist is a modeler known as 'Mr. Tebo,' who worked at a number of factories. He used an impressed mark, T^o, on much of his work, and the plates show a number of specimens thus marked. Very little is known of him, and he first appears in the records as being employed by Wedgwood in 1774. There is also an advertisement in the *Daily Advertiser* in 1747 which refers to 'Mr. Teboe,' a jeweler. It is probable that, like so many artists in England at the time, he was a Huguenot, originally Thibaud or Thibault, and that his name had been spelled phonetically for so long that he adopted it as he had adopted his new country.

The collected body of work marked with the *Tº*, from whatever factory it comes, is coherent and related. The mark first appears on some salts decorated with marine shells made at Bow some time between 1750 and 1755, and a Bow cormorant is similarly decorated with shells on the base. The mark also appears on a group of small boys playing musical instruments in the Katz Collection, and this has a shell-encrusted base. It certainly appears on the Worcester vase illustrated on Plate 170 which has a phoenix as a finial, and this bird not only closely resembles the cormorant mentioned, but also the eagle on which Zeus is mounted (Plate 132). The style of modeling to be seen in the figure of Zeus is not only the same as with the group of small boys already referred to, but is similar to that of the figure surmounting the clockcase shown in Plate 138, which bears the mark of Tebo.

Some of the very rare figures from Worcester which seem to be modeled by a familiar Bow hand also bear his mark, and although the figures appearing on Plate 153 are not marked, the stylistic resemblance is equally strong.

Mr. Tebo is thought to have worked at Plymouth, where his sign manual appears. Some Plymouth models closely resemble those from Bow, and the familiar hand is to be seen once again in the pair of phoenixes which are illustrated on Plate 156.

In the early part of the 1760s, Bow experienced some financial trouble which, no doubt, caused Tebo to move on elsewhere. It is difficult to be certain of his destination, but it seems likely that he went to Plymouth first, and then to Worcester. The Plymouth factory was started by William Cookworthy in 1768, and the factory at Worcester was making figures in 1771, when Mrs. Phillipp Lybbe Powys visited it. This they had not done previously. It is probable that he arrived in Bristol about 1772, but he seems to have modeled no figures for this factory, and to have functioned principally as a vase-maker. Some Bristol vases very closely resemble those bearing his mark from Worcester.

His employment with Wedgwood was of short duration, and he was principally employed in roughing out figures for others to finish. He later went to Dublin, where we finally lose sight of him.

I have examined the problem of Tebo at some length because it illustrates admirably the way in which the history of English porcelain has been pieced together. Unlike the great Continental factories, the archives of these English undertakings are sadly lacunary, and often there is little more than the wares themselves on which to base a reconstruction.

In the case of Bow we have a number of documentary sources, including the notebooks of John Bowcocke, clerk to the factory, and several contemporary newspaper advertisements. Many of the gaps, however, have been filled in by deductions made in precisely this way.

Two important early Bow figures by an unknown hand are portraits of the actress, Kitty Clive, and her companion, Henry Woodward, illustrated on Plate 128. The origin of these is discussed in the caption, but it is appropriate to say here that some very rare contemporary copies of Kitty Clive exist on plain bases, and in a body which does not contain bone ash. An attribution to the factory at Longton

Hall, in Staffordshire, has been suggested. Bow made a number of figures from the theatre of the time, including the figure of Falstaff (Plate 127) which is discussed in some detail on the caption to the plate.

The factory experienced difficult times which started with the retirement of Thomas Frye in 1759. Weatherby died in 1762, and Crowther became bankrupt in the following year. Bow continued working on a much reduced scale, and these later wares have little of the artistry of the former production. Figures, in particular, tend to be garishly colored. It closed finally in 1778.

It is, perhaps, appropriate at this point to discuss the origin of the English practice of transfer printing which was but rarely used on the Continent before the 19th century. Technically, it is a comparatively simple matter. An engraved copperplate was inked with ceramic color, and an impression taken on paper. Whilst the ink was still wet it was pressed on the surface to be decorated, and the ware was then fired to fix the color in the usual way. Such prints were made under the glaze in blue, or over the glaze in black, purple, or brick red. Blue and black printing was most commonly done.

The invention, claimed by Sadler & Green of Liverpool, is, perhaps, most reliably attributed to John Brooks, an Irish engraver and friend of Thomas Frye. A small amount of printing was done at Bow, and at the enamel works in Battersea, in south London. One or two isolated specimens of Chelsea porcelain printed in blue have been noted.

The most important practitioner of this kind of work was Robert Hancock, discussed later in considering the Worcester factory. Hancock first worked for Bow, traveling to Worcester about 1757.

DERBY (DERBYSHIRE)

THERE IS REASON to think that Thomas Briand, in company with James Marchand, attempted to start a factory at Derby about 1745. There is also mention in contemporary records of a potter named André Planché, who may have worked about the same date. It is impossible to say what, if anything, they made. There are some small white cream jugs, one of which is known with 'Derby' incised, one bears a simple script 'D,' and one (in the Victoria and Albert Museum) is marked 'D 1750.' These are allied to a class of figures, extremely well-modeled, which exhibit a certain amount of glaze retraction at the base, and often have a funnel-shaped hole in addition. This class is represented on Plates 122 and 123 by some distinguished pieces of modeling, but little is otherwise known of them, or of their origin. They appear to imitate some of the Chelsea red anchor figures in style, and were made between 1750 and 1755.

In 1750 William Duesbury, the son of a tanner of Cannock, in Staffordshire, was operating a decorating establishment in London. From his surviving account books it is possible to say that he was enameling white porcelain from Bow, Chelsea, Longton Hall, and Derby, as well as salt glaze from Staffordshire. At this time the art of enameling was not well understood at the factories, and Duesbury was much in demand. In 1749 the Duc de Luynes was able to write:

'The English order (from France) only the porcelain in a white glazed state so that they can paint it themselves.'

In a very few years, however, the factories had mastered the art of enameling, and Duesbury's services were no longer in demand. It is probable that he found, like the *Hausmaler* of Germany before him, that factories became less willing to supply him with white porcelain, and he therefore took the logical step of deciding to make his own.

In 1756 he returned to the Midlands, and was actively negotiating with Planché, and with John Heath, to found a new factory in Derby. John Heath was the moving spirit in a factory at Cockpit Hill, Derby, which made salt glaze, creamware, and such things, and this factory may, in fact, have been responsible for the 'dry-edged' class already mentioned. Duesbury obtained capital from his father, who transferred all his property to his son in exchange for an annuity. This was faithfully paid until the elder man's death in 1768.

In the *Public Advertiser* in 1756 we find the following advertisement:

'To be Sold by auction by Mr. Bellamy by order of the Proprietors of the Derby Porcelain Manufactory ... A curious collection of fine figures, jars, sauceboats, services for deserts (dessert), and a great variety of other useful and ornamental porcelains after the finest Dresden (Meissen) models, all exquisitely painted and enamelled with flowers, insects, India plants, &c.'

And in 1757, Duesbury was advertising himself as 'Derby, or the second Dresden,' and goes on to say that 'many good judges could not distinguish (this porcelain) from the real Dresden.'

Derby figures of this period are never marked, and it may be that Duesbury hoped to pass them off as the work of Chelsea or Meissen. If this was, indeed, his intention, he succeeded very well. Derby figures were, for many years, confused with later Chelsea productions, and the difference was only discerned when Bernard Rackham pointed out that Derby figures almost always bore three 'patch' marks on the base, about the size of a thumbprint, which marked the pads on which they had rested in the kiln. The superb example illustrated on Plate 140 is the exception which proves the rule. This is marked on the base 'WDCo,' and is, I think, the only marked example known at this period. It is, however, documentary to the extent that it confirms the attribution of the unmarked examples.

From 1756 until 1770 production was on a large scale, and progressively increased. For a few years, during the financial troubles of Bow and the illness of Sprimont, Derby was almost the only source of porcelain figures in England, a circumstance which no doubt led the Worcester factory, who had hitherto only made service ware, to make a few figures about 1770.

In 1770 Duesbury purchased the moribund factory at Chelsea, and production at the two factories was now combined. Six bags of bone ash went from Chelsea to Derby, and Duesbury began to experiment with a phosphatic body. In addition, he opened showrooms in London.

Production at Chelsea was discontinued in 1784 and perhaps for the last few years it was little more than a decorating establishment, similar to the one owned by Wedgwood not far away.

After 1770 the productions of Duesbury began to show the influence of the prevailing neo-classical style which had been brought to England by the Brothers Adam, architects and interior decorators. The severe and formal lines of the new fashion were more easily transposed into the creamware of Wedgwood, but Derby neo-classicism is, perhaps, more acceptable than most essays in this style from the porcelain factories of Europe. Duesbury reverted to his earlier love of enameling, and gathered about him a group of painters of uncommon merit. Perhaps foremost among them was Zachariah Boreman, a Chelsea artist who probably did the birds on the Mecklenburg-Strelitz service. Boreman was a painter of landscape of great skill, whose technique owes much to the influence of the noted Derby water-colorist, Paul Sandby. Another of Sandby's pupils, Robert Brewer, also painted landscapes for Derby late in the 18th century.

James Banfield did figure subjects, and his work is frequently to be found on the reverse of such things as vases with Boreman landscapes. He also painted birds, landscapes, and flowers, but with an ill grace, and in a letter to Duesbury in 1795 he writes: 'You must know, sir, people are not camelions (chameleons), and that reward sweetens labour.'

Of exceptional importance is William Billingsley, who was apprenticed to the factory in 1774. His father was in business as a japanner and painter, and may at one time have worked at Chelsea as a flower painter. Billingsley's most important work can be found in his flower painting, which excelled in quality and naturalism anything of the kind which was being done at the time. Characteristic is a long spray which emerges from the central grouping, and a fondness for white flowers. His color was put on in a full wash, and the highlights were then removed with a dry brush. An example of his work appears on Plate 144.

So highly was Billingsley regarded that when Joseph Lygo, the factory's London agent, heard that he had quarrelled with Duesbury he wrote:

'I hope you will be able to make a bargain with Mr. Billingsley for him to continue with you, for it will be a great loss to lose such a hand, and not only that, but his going to another factory will put them in the way of doing flowers in the same way, which at present they are entirely ignorant of.'

Despite this, he left in 1796, and later opened a porcelain factory of his own at Nantgarw, in South Wales, which for a time made superb porcelain, but was commercially unsuccessful. His style was extensively copied by other artists.

From its inception the Derby factory of Duesbury made figures in great variety. A list of the contents of 42 boxes sent to London for sale in 1763 refers both to figures which can be identified, and to those which remain to be discovered, if, indeed, they still exist. John Haslem, formerly at the factory, gave at length a price list of about 1795 in his book, *The Old Derby China Factory*, published in 1876. This is a useful list, because each model is given a reference number which often appears incised on the base. Many were made in more than one size, and this, too, is recorded. In this way, it is possible not only to identify many of the models, but also the size, and, in some cases, the modeler.

A word of caution is necessary in reference to one particular entry – the so-called *Mansion House Dwarfs*. These, first modeled about 1784, are said to have been taken from two dwarfs who stood at the Mansion House in London, but they are actually close copies of grotesque figures derived from Jacques Callot, and are almost identical with a model from Mennecy made some thirty years earlier. These dwarfs have been reproduced on the Continent in fairly large quantities, and are a good deal more common than the genuine specimens.

Many reproductions of this kind are replete with false marks, and this is, perhaps, a suitable point at which to repeat the warning given many years ago by Emil Hannover, that the most certain way to get together a bad collection is to rely on marks. The marks of all European factories of any importance have been repeated on reproductions, and a mark is never, in any circumstances, to be regarded as the sole test of authenticity. The Chelsea anchor, the Meissen crossed swords, and the Royal Monogram of Sèvres, have all been persistently abused in this way, but many of the smaller factories, such as Derby, are hardly in better case.

Of the modelers who worked at Derby, there is record of figures being supplied by John Bacon, R. A., and Duesbury paid him £75 in 1769 for work done. Plate 112, the central figure of three groups taken from a portrait of the Royal family by Zoffany, which was made in 1773, is likely to have been by him, and figures of Milton and Shakespeare (Nos. 297 and 305 in the price list) were probably his work.

A Frenchman, Pierre Stephan, also worked for Duesbury at the factory for about four years, between 1770 and 1774, and later supplied him with models as a free lance. It was probably he who did three well-known groups – No. 195 (*Two Virgins Awakening Cupid*), No. 196 (*Two Bacchantes adorning Pan*), and No. 235 (*Three Graces distressing Cupid*) – after paintings by Angelica Kauffman, a Swiss artist who became a member of the Royal Academy.

Jean-Jacques Spengler, son of the director of the Zurich factory, worked at Derby, although most attributions to him are conjectural. William Coffee also modeled at Derby after 1794, and the best known example of his work is No. 396, a Shepherd, which is a clothed copy of an antique statue of Adonis.

The factory did much work in *biscuit* porcelain, and slightly defective models of this kind were often glazed and painted to make them salable. Any particular model, therefore, is likely to be found in either version.

114. PEASANT. BOW PORCELAIN. C. 1750

Height 23 cm. Collection: Major-General Sir Harold Wernher, Bart., Luton Hoo, Bedfordshire

Perhaps a figure of an itinerant seller; this is suggested by the staff and gaiters. The hand is that of the 'Muses Modeler,' who is more familiar as the artist responsible for some early figures of the Muses (see page 165). The face, in particular, is typical of his style — oval, with a slightly receding chin. The coloring, too, is characteristic, especially that of the face. The base is a slight mound, free of scrollwork, and this type was invariably used in the early period, the higher, *rococo*, bases (Plate 118) being introduced towards 1758. Plate 126 – the Muse, Urania – is by the same hand, and here the face may be seen in profile, illustrating the receding chin characteristic of this man's work.

---

115. AN ITALIAN COMEDY GROUP. BOW PORCELAIN. C. 1755

21 cm. The Syndics of the Fitzwilliam Museum, Cambridge

This rare group is a close copy of *The Indiscreet Harlequin*, a model by J.J. Kändler at Meissen which belongs to the magnificent series of Harlequin subjects done by him between 1740 and 1745. The Meissen base with applied flowers has been faithfully reproduced, and the group testifies to the popularity of Meissen porcelain in England at the time.

---

116. JUG. BOW PORCELAIN. C. 1755

21 cm. The Brighton Art Gallery and Museum (Willett Collection), Brighton, Sussex

This very rare jug represents a parson carousing outside an inn with friends. The look of insobriety on the faces of the party has been well caught by the artist. It is uncertain whether the sign (a pair of oxhorns) has the traditional significance. It may be connected with a custom of 'swearing on the horns' observed at certain inns at Highgate, to the North of London, which were much frequented by cattle drovers in the 18th century. Those who swore the oath and kissed the horns were made freemen of the inn, which carried with it the privilege of kicking a pig out of a ditch and taking her place when the freeman wanted to rest. He was warned, however, that if he saw three pigs lying together, he was only entitled to kick out the middle one and to lie between the other two. Parsons seem to have been noted for insobriety in the 18th century, as witness the group on Plate 70.

---

117. PEACOCK AND PEAHEN. BOW PORCELAIN. C. 1756

18 cm. Collection: Major-General Sir Harold Wernher, Bart., Luton Hoo, Bedfordshire

This pair of birds, inspired by those of Kändler at Meissen, are fully equal to Chelsea in quality. The porcelain body is pure white and glassy, whilst the coloring is of the utmost brilliance. It is rare to find work of this kind from Bow, which was much more concerned to fill the demand for medium quality wares. They must, therefore, be regarded as exceptional.

114

115

117

119

120

122

123

125

118. PARROTS. BOW PORCELAIN. C. 1758

19 cm. Collection: Major-General Sir Harold Wernher, Bart., Luton Hoo, Bedfordshire

These gaily colored parrots are similar to those of Kändler at Meissen modeled about 1733, but the *rococo* bases have been added as a concession to the prevailing fashion. These bases are typical of those to be seen on many Bow figures of the period, although they later became more clumsy and less refined in design. The parrots of Kändler were observed at the Moritzburg aviaries of Augustus the Strong, to which he frequently resorted for inspiration, and aviaries had been popular in Europe from the time of Diane de Poitiers at the Château d'Anet.

119. PLATE. BOW PORCELAIN. C. 1758

Diameter 23 cm. The Trustees of the Cecil Higgins Museum, Bedford

This plate has the characteristic recessed base which marks it at once as coming from Bow. The porcelain is virtually opaque, which is probably the result of firing at a slightly lower temperature than that needed for complete vitrification. The chocolate edge is a survival from the earlier imitations of Japanese porcelain by Kakiemon, and the botanical decoration is by a well-known hand responsible for similar work at Chelsea during the red anchor period. The subject is taken from illustrations to the work of Philip Miller, and decoration of this kind is usually referred to as 'Hans Sloane' flowers (see page 127).

120. BOWL FOR POTPOURRI. BOW PORCELAIN. C. 1758

25.4 cm. The Victoria and Albert Museum (Schreiber Collection), London

This unusual covered potpourri bowl is obviously copied from a silver original as the gadrooning, and the form of the foot, clearly show. The piercing, too, outlines *rococo* scrolls, and owes a good deal to similar work in silver. The piper surmounting the cover is adapted from a bronze by Giovanni da Bologna, and a version is also known in tin-enameled ware from Delft, in Holland. The mark is T^o impressed, for Mr. Tebo, and it is possible that he modeled the surmounting figure. The custom of using figures as knops in this way was, of course, quite common in silver and metalwork generally, and it was much used in porcelain at Meissen and Vienna.

121. THE MARQUIS OF GRANBY. BOW PORCELAIN. C. 1759

Height 37 cm. The Brighton Museum and Art Gallery (Willett Collection), Brighton, Sussex

This (and items illustrated elsewhere) comes from a collection of English pottery and porcelain illustrating British history which was bequeathed to the Brighton Museum by Henry Willett. General John Manners, the Marquis of Granby (b. 1721–d. 1770), wears the uniform of a Colonel of the Horse Guards, an appointment he received in 1758. This figure was probably made to commemorate the Battle of Minden in 1759, one of the engagements of the Seven Years' War in which the Duke of Brunswick (Plate 177) was victorious over the French armies. The figure illustrated was adapted from the well-known portrait by Sir Joshua Reynolds, engraved by Richard Houston. It was probably modeled by Tebo.

122. CHINOISERIE GROUP. DERBY PORCELAIN. C. 1750

23 cm. Collection: Major-General Sir Harold Wernher, Bart., Luton Hoo, Bedfordshire

A fine example of early Derby figure modeling before the advent of Duesbury. This group belongs to the 'dry-edged' class, and is a derivation from the *chinoiseries* of Boucher by way of Meissen. The vigor and skill in modeling which characterizes most of these figures can well be seen. It should be compared with Plate 123.

123. GRAPE SELLERS. DERBY PORCELAIN. C. 1751

18.5 cm. Collection: Major-General Sir Harold Wernher, Bart., Luton Hoo, Bedfordshire

These two rare and distinguished examples of English figure modeling belong to the so-called 'dry-edged' class of early Derby porcelain. The primary inspiration is almost certainly Continental, but they have a particular attraction of their own in the soft porcelain body. The glaze retraction from the base can be well seen just below the shoes of the male figure. These were probably enameled by William Duesbury at his studio in London, and 'Darbyshire figars' frequently appear in his account book as having been painted by him.

124. SWEETMEAT STAND. DERBY PORCELAIN. C. 1760

38.5 cm. The Trustees of the Cecil Higgins Museum, Bedford

A popular form of sweetmeat stand made at Derby, and at several other English porcelain factories. This example, of extremely large size, has been made in two parts. The carefully modeled marine shells, corals, and the like are a typical early *rococo* theme. This style was much concerned with water as a subject, one of the earliest *rococo* porcelain services in Europe being the 'Swan' service from Meissen which was entirely based on aquatic themes.

125. TEAPOT. DERBY PORCELAIN. C. 1790

14 cm. The Victoria and Albert Museum (Herbert Allen Collection), London

Teapot, with a pale pink ground, painted with landscapes within a gilt striped border by Zachariah Boreman. Another landscape by the same hand is on the reverse. The scenes are titled inside the footring in blue enamel, the view shown being 'On the Trent, Derbyshire' (pattern number 231). Boreman was the foremost painter of landscapes at Derby during the latter part of the 18th century, and the practice of naming the scene represented was common from the end of the 18th century onwards. Such paintings are often referred to as 'Named Views.'

126   127

128

129

133

134

136

137 138

139

141

142

143

145

126. URANIA. BOW PORCELAIN. C. 1750

15 cm. The Hastings Art Gallery and Museum, Hastings, Sussex

Urania, the Muse of Astronomy, is shown measuring the globe with dividers. It is from the hand of the 'Muses Modeller,' and it is typical of the work of this unknown artist who is further discussed on Plate 114 and page 165. He may have been of French extraction – it is possible to infer this from an inscription on the base of a figure of the Muse, Erato. The Muses were goddesses who presided over different aspects of poetry, the arts, and the sciences.

127. FALSTAFF. BOW PORCELAIN. C. 1750

24 cm. The Victoria and Albert Museum (Schreiber Collection), London

This figure is perhaps intended to represent the Irish actor, James Quin, as Falstaff. It was taken from the central figure of an engraving made in 1743 by G. Grignion, after a painting by Francis Hayman, entitled *Falstaff's Cowardice Detected*. This figure is sometimes said to have been derived from an engraving by James McArdell, but Mander and Mitchenson have shown that this engraving is probably spurious, McArdell's name having been added later by the contemporary print seller, Sayer, to an untitled plate.

Quin excelled in the character of Falstaff, but retired from the stage in 1750, probably because he had lost his front teeth. To an invitation to play the part in 1754, he replied: 'I will whistle Falstaff for no one.' Quin had an irascible temperament, and was twice involved in duels. Nevertheless, he was generous with money, and was extremely popular. He was associated with Peg Woffington (Plate 129) in a number of productions.

128. HENRY WOODWARD AND KITTY CLIVE. BOW PORCELAIN C. 1750

27 cm. The Trustees of the Cecil Higgins Museum, Bedford

Woodward, on the left, is in the character of the Fine Gentleman from Garrick's farce, *Lethe*. Kitty Clive, right, is the Fine Lady. The Woodward figure is from an engraving by James McArdell after a painting by Francis Hayman, and Kitty Clive is based on an engraving by Charles Mosley, perhaps after a water color by Worledge. The known figures of Woodward all appear to come from Bow, but a small number of specimens of Kitty Clive are in a non-phosphatic body and may have been made either at Longton Hall or Derby. The suggestion that the model was made at Chelsea is credible, particularly as a pair of Chelsea sphinxes exist which have the head of the figure illustrated here, but the non-phosphatic specimens I have been able to examine were not typical of Chelsea porcelain. It has also been suggested that the lack of phosphatic reaction is due to the fact that some of these models were made at Bow before the introduction of bone ash into the body, but an examination of the 1744 patent suggests that a phosphatic reaction could be expected from any porcelain made in this way also. The figure of Kitty Clive, therefore, is one of the minor mysteries of English porcelain which time may resolve.

Kitty Rafter was noticed by Colley Cibber, manager of Drury Lane theatre in 1727, and enjoyed great success as an actress and singer. She married a barrister, George Clive, but they separated soon after the ceremony. Another version from Bow is on a high base with molded trophies on the front.

---

129. SPHINX. BOW PORCELAIN. C. 1750

12.5 cm. The Victoria and Albert Museum (Schreiber Collection), London

One of a pair. The head is probably intended as a portrait of Peg Woffington, the actress, and is apparently adapted from a painting by Arthur Pond, engraved by McArdell. This portrait is in the National Portrait Gallery in London.

Peg Woffington, an Irish actress, made her debut at Covent Garden in 1740. She also acted with Garrick (Plate 155) with whom she lived for several years. She sometimes played male parts, notably that of Sir Harry Wildair in *The Constant Couple*, which led to an amusing and barbed interchange between herself and Garrick. After a performance she remarked: 'Half the men in London believe me to be a man.' To which he replied: 'Madam, the other half know you to be a woman.'

The origin of the curious form taken by this portrait is interesting. The grotesques of Raphael, so-called because he took them from grottoes in the rediscovered Golden House of Nero, were used by the French designer, Jean Bérain, and somewhat similar figures to this one appear in tapestries and such things designed by him. It became fashionable for ladies of the French court to have their portraits made in this form, at first in *terracotta* and later in porcelain. The fashion crossed the Channel, and although the model shown is the most frequent survival, it does appear in other forms (Plate 100).

---

130. SEATED HOUND. BOW PORCELAIN. C. 1753

9.25 cm. Collection: Major-General Sir Harold Wernher, Bart., Luton Hoo, Bedfordshire

This hound, one of a pair, is seated in a dismal pose. The markings are finely lined in brown, and the nose and toes are black. The flowers on the base are conventionally colored. Bow made a number of dogs of all sorts, and whilst this is not the rarest, it is the most appealing.

---

131. NUN. BOW PORCELAIN. C. 1755

14 cm. Collection: W. R. B. Young, Esq., St. Leonards-on-Sea, Sussex

Derived from a Meissen model of a *Heilige Frau* of about 1750, the costume has been simplified and the headdress is slightly less elaborate. The pose, too, is a little more restrained and less *baroque* in feeling. Generally, however, the differences are not great. The base is of the early variety, and slightly later versions have a *rococo* scroll base. They appear to have been made for devotional purposes, and she carries a breviary marked 'Omnia gloria....' The hood is enameled black, and the robe is puce and white.

132. ZEUS. BOW PORCELAIN. C. 1755

17 cm. Collection: W. R. B. Young, Esq., St. Leonards-on-Sea, Sussex

This amusing figure is Air from a set representing the Elements. Zeus wears a puce cloak with a blue lining, and his thunderbolt is yellow tipped with orange-red. His black socks are held in position by what appear to be gold garters, and may have been added to cover underlying faults in the glaze. The eagle, on which Zeus is mounted, strongly resembles the modeling of the birds shown on Plates 156 and 170, and this figure is probably from the hand of Mr. Tebo. The base represents clouds.

133. COOKS. BOW PORCELAIN. C. 1755

17 cm. Collection: Major-General Sir Harold Wernher, Bart., Luton Hoo, Bedfordshire

The woman wears a puce coat with yellow cuffs and blue collar. The bodice of her gown is black, and her shoes are black with blue flowers. The man wears a black soft cap, black shoes, and pale yellow breeches. The painted flowers are in red, blue, and green, and those on the base are conventionally colored. The figures have an impressed mark, *B*, at one time thought to be the initial of John Bacon, R.A., to whom they were assigned. This is extremely doubtful, but they are distinguished examples of figure modeling which are among the best things to come from the factory.

134. PEDDLER. BOW PORCELAIN. C. 1755

17 cm. Collection: Major-General Sir Harold Wernher, Bart., Luton Hoo, Bedfordshire

The figure has cap and cuffs of enamel blue which is a characteristic Bow color. The waistcoat and breeches are decorated with flowers in blue, puce, yellow, and green, the gaiters are colored puce, and the shoes, black. The flowers on the base are the same as those on the dress. This figure is extremely similar to a small bronze in the Victoria and Albert Museum, from which it appears to have been derived.

135. TEAPOT. BOW PORCELAIN. C. 1756

19 cm. The Victoria and Albert Museum (Schreiber Collection), London

This teapot is decorated with a half-length portrait of Frederick the Great of Prussia copied from a painting by Antoine Pesne, and engraved by J. G. Wille. It is a transfer print carried out in purplish-brown, and above, to the left, is a print of a figure representing Fame, whilst to the right, a winged *putto* bears a laurel wreath. The cover is printed with trophies of arms, and the molded flowers around the junction of the handle and on the cover are painted in the usual enamel colors. This teapot seems to have been made slightly before the Worcester version of the same subject in 1757. Frederick was exceedingly popular in England at the time (the beginning of the Seven Years' War). In 1758 Walpole wrote in a letter: 'All England kept his birthday. It has taken its place in our calendar next to Admiral Vernon's and my Lord Blakeney's, and the people, I believe, think that Prussia is part of Old England.'

136. WATERMAN. BOW PORCELAIN. C. 1758

24 cm. Brighton Art Gallery and Museum (Willett Collection), Brighton, Sussex

The waterman is sometimes said to wear Doggett's Coat and Badge, a prize founded in 1715 by an Irish actor, Thomas Doggett, in honor of the accession to the throne of George I. Each year, on August 1st, a race was held for Thames watermen which started at London Bridge and finished at Chelsea. The winner was awarded a coat of red, and a large silver arm badge. The custom still exists, and since 1791 a note has been kept of the name of the winner. Red was a color to use successfully, and the figure wears a canary yellow coat, a blue scarf, and brown difficult breeches. The base, which is characteristic of Bow figures of the period, is picked out with puce and blue enamels. The figure exists in an earlier version on a plain base.

137. MUG. BOW PORCELAIN. C. 1758

21.5 cm. The Victoria and Albert Museum (Schreiber Collection), London

This bell-shaped mug has, on the front, the crest of a goat's head *erased* surrounded by gilt scrollwork. The remainder of the painted decoration is based on Kakiemon patterns. The cover is surmounted by a pug dog derived from a model by Kändler at Meissen.

138. WATCH STAND. BOW PORCELAIN. C. 1759

33 cm. The Trustees of the Cecil Higgins Museum, Bedford

This most interesting specimen is dated 1757 and 1759, but the latter year is the more likely. It is marked with an impressed T^o, signifying the hand of Tebo, and the surmounting figure is stylistically similar to Zeus (Plate 132). The painting of sheet music links it with some rare specimens similarly decorated which are also dated 1759, and one of these bears the inscription 'To great handle the god of musick, 1759.' It seems likely that all were made as a tribute to the composer, George Frederick Handel, at the time of his death on the 14th April, 1759. The one shown is decorated with various initials – GH (twice repeated) AC, and IH, and numbers (17278 and 0721). The sheet music bears several titles – *The Flye, York tune, Minuet, Sally*, and *Air*. The scrollwork is colored in puce and blue, a typical Bow color scheme, with touches of yellow and green. On the reverse, the enameler has accidentally left his thumbprint in blue enamel. The origin of this example appears to be Meissen. The surmounting figure is not unlike the work of Eberlein, and several Bow models which can be reasonably attributed to Tebo had their origin in the work of this Meissen artist.

139. VASE. DERBY. C. 1758

29 cm. The Hastings Museum and Art Gallery, Hastings, Sussex

This vase has a deep sponged blue ground, with exotic birds and flowers painted in panels reserved in white. There is some oil gilding. On the handles there are touches of 'dirty' turquoise, a color particularly associated with Derby at this period. This is a naive provincial derivation from Sèvres.

140. BAGPIPER. DERBY PORCELAIN. C. 1760

28.5 cm. The British Museum, London

The quality of this figure is proof that Duesbury's claim to be regarded as the 'second Dresden' was not entirely without foundation. It bears the mark 'WDCo' incised on the base, and is the only existing specimen known to be thus inscribed. Until 1770, when Duesbury acquired the Chelsea factory, none of his products bore a factory mark, although specimens marked with a Chelsea anchor are sometimes to be seen. The conclusion that he endeavored to pass off his products as coming from such factories as Chelsea and Meissen is inescapable.

141. COWS. DERBY PORCELAIN. C. 1763

8 cm. Hastings Museum and Art Gallery, Hastings, Sussex

The bases are floral, the flowers being touched with puce. The cows have orange-red markings, and the hoofs are black. Distantly derived from the Meissen cows of Kändler, these are typically English in feeling.

142. TITHE PIG GROUP. DERBY PORCELAIN. C. 1765

17.5 cm. The Victoria and Albert Museum (Schreiber Collection), London

Tithe was a tenth part of farm produce compulsorily taken by the Established Church for its upkeep. The injustice of this tax, levied indiscriminately regardless of religious belief, has always been a cause of unrest and discontent among English farmers upon whom it falls. The present group, satirical in intent, represents a farmer's wife determined not to part with the tenth pig unless the parson takes the tenth child. It probably illustrates the contemporary verse which follows:

'The Parson comes, the Pig he Claims,
And the good Wife with Taunts inflames,
But she quite Arch bow'd low and smiled,
Kept back the Pig and held the Child.
The Priest look'd gruff, the Wife look'd big,
Zounds, Sir, quothe she, no Child, no Pig.'

There are many 18th century references which testify to the bitterness of feeling on the subject. It appears as a transfer-print on creamware, and a figure of the parson, modeled separately, is to be found among Ralph Wood earthenware figures bearing the inscription:

'I will have no child tho the y pig.'

143. JEAN-JACQUES ROUSSEAU. DERBY PORCELAIN. C. 1775

16.5 cm. The Victoria and Albert Museum (Schreiber Collection), London

This bust of Rousseau is based on a portrait painted by J. H. Taraval, and engraved by C. H. Watelet in 1766, from a bronze medal of 1761 by Leclerc. Rousseau, here shown in Armenian costume with a fur cap, spent four years in England from 1766 at the invitation of the philosopher, David Hume. A similar bust was made in creamware, probably by Enoch Wood of Burslem. He wears a brown coat and puce cloak, and there are touches of gilding.

---

144. FLOWER VASE. DERBY PORCELAIN. C. 1790

20.5 cm. The Victoria and Albert Museum (Herbert Allen Collection), London

Vase and stand, the latter with two partly gilded loop handles with foliate molding at the junction. The oval panel has a bouquet of flowers superbly painted by William Billingsley (see page 169). At the top the flowers are predominantly white (a Billingsley characteristic), those in the middle are light mauve and pink, with orange-red at the bottom. The ground is dark blue, enriched with *vermiculé* gilding derived from Sèvres.

---

145. LIBERTY AND MATRIMONY. RALPH WOOD'S PORCELAIN STAFFORDSHIRE. C. 1785

28 cm. The Victoria and Albert Museum (Gift: W. T. Lee, Esq.), London

The subject of this group was commonly used in England by a number of factories during the 18th century and later for groups and pairs of figures. The example illustrated is extremely rare, very few specimens of Ralph Wood porcelain having been identified. It is characteristic of pottery groups from the same source. Like them, it is light in weight and hollow cast in slip. The figures are colored with green, puce, orange-red, mauve, blue, and black enamels. The modeling is unsophisticated in comparison with that of the porcelain factories of the period.

THE ORIGIN of the Worcester factory may have been in a small unsuccessful undertaking at Limehouse, in the East End of London. Dr. Richard Pococke, who kept a journey of his travels through England, wrote of his stay in Bristol in 1750:

'I went to see the manufacture lately established here by one of the principal of the manufacture at Limehouse which failed. It is at a glass-house and is called Lowris' China House.'

He refers to china made from calcined flint and soapy rock (soaprock or steatite) from Lizard Point in Cornwall, and this inclusion of soaprock is a characteristic of porcelain made both at Bristol at this time, and at Worcester to which the undertaking was later transferred.

The undertaker at Bristol was a Quaker named Benjamin Lund, who was given a licence to mine soaprock at Lizard Point in 1748. It is possible that William Cookworthy of Plymouth, already mentioned in reference to the use of Virginian china clay, had some kind of connection with this factory. For the most part this is assumption, based on the fact that he was searching in Cornwall for the ingredients of porcelain, and that both he and Lund were Quakers, but there is a statement made much later by Sarah Champion that Cookworthy was the 'first inventor of the Bristol china ware' which, from the context, may refer to this early factory.

The Bristol factory was established at Redcliff Backs in a glassworks formerly owned by a man named Lowdin, and the 'Lowris' referred to by Pococke is an obvious mishearing of 'Lowdins.' It can, I think, be assumed that it started work in 1748, and some figures copied from the *blanc de Chine* of Tê Hua, marked *Bristoll 1750* on the back in relief, are obviously documentary. A fairly common survival are some silver-pattern sauceboats with an outcurving lip. The glaze is slightly blue in tone, and has an opaque appearance which may be due to an addition of a small amount of tin oxide – likely enough at a center for the manufacture of delft such as Bristol. These are often painted with Chinese scenes in enamel colors based on the Ch'ing dynasty *famille verte* and *famille rose*. Parenthetically, it is worth observing here that whereas other English factories derived most of their Oriental patterns from Japan, these were rarely used at Worcester. Instead, patterns based on Chinese originals, and, in some cases, copies as may be seen from Plate 160, are the rule. An example of this kind of work at Bristol is shown on Plate 157, but some of these things are repeated soon after the factory's transference to Worcester, and the line of demarcation is not always clear. They are then referred to as 'Bristol-Worcester' – an indication that they might have been made at either place.

In Felix Farley's *Bristol Journal* for the 24th July, 1752, and again on the 8th August of that year, we find the following advertisement:

'Whereas the proprietors of the Manufactory for making (china) ware in this City... are now united with the Worcester Porcelain Company, where for the future, the whole business will be carried on; therefore the said Proprietors are determin'd to sell the remaining Stock of Ware very cheap at their Warehouse in Castle Green until the whole is disposed of.'

The Worcester Company was actually formed in 1751, the four principal shareholders being William Bayliss, Richard Holdship, Edward Cave (editor of the *Gentleman's Magazine*), and Josiah Holdship. Dr. John Wall and William Davis were also shareholders to the value of £225 apiece – about half the amount held by Josiah Holdship. The largest investment (£675) was subscribed by William Bayliss. Wall and Davis were given an amount equivalent to their combined shareholding for their part in acquiring the secret of manufacture, and special payment was made to two Bristol workmen, Robert Podmore and John Lyes.

Perhaps in recognition of their predilection for Chinese styles, the new factory called itself the Worcester Tonquin Manufactory, and, by March, 1753, it had opened a warehouse in London for the sale of its products. Among the early productions may be found a silver-pattern sauceboat also manufactured at Bristol. At the earlier factory, the mark *Bristoll* was sometimes used, raised in relief, and a specimen is known from Worcester marked *Wigornia* in the same way. This is a variant of the Latin form of Worcester – *Vigornium*.

For some years Worcester retained its liking for decoration in the Chinese manner, and the first real departure may be noted in 1757 when Robert Hancock, the engraver, arrived from Bow, bringing the secret of transfer printing. Many of the earlier Worcester wares decorated in this way have the mark of Hancock, 'RH,' together with an anchor – a rebus on the name, *Holdship*. Richard Holdship is thought to have been in charge of the printing department, and evidence of a sharp clash between the two men is provided by a verse printed in the *Gentleman's Magazine* for December, 1757, in reference to Hancock's popular print of Frederick the Great:

'What praise is thine, ingenious Holdship, who
On the fair porcelain the portrait drew –
To thee, who first, in thy judicious mind,
A perfect model of the art designed –
On which, long by curious artists sought,
By thee alone to great perfection's brought.'

In the *Worcester Journal* for January, 1758, the first two lines were repeated, with this addition –

'Hancock, my friend, don't grieve tho' Holdship has the praise.
Tis yours to execute, tis his to wear the bays.'

This did but rough justice to Hancock, but, in 1759, Richard Holdship left Worcester, and offered the secret of soaprock porcelain and transfer printing to Duesbury at Derby. The latter, so far as can be ascertained, made no use of the soaprock formula, but a few specimens of Derby porcelain and cream-ware decorated with transfer prints have been recorded. Hancock prints on Worcester porcelain are now much sought by collectors. Most are either in black or in underglaze blue, although red and lilac transfers can be noticed occasionally. He became a partner in 1772, and in 1774 went to a small factory at Caughley in Shropshire which made useful wares in the style of Worcester.

Soon after 1760 the factory began to make wares decorated with a ground of small overlapping scales in underglaze blue – the so-called 'scale-blue' ground. These had reserved panels left in white in which painting in enamel colors could be executed. Much ware of the kind was sold to James Giles who had a decorating studio in Kentish Town in London. Although we do not know when it started, this studio was in existence in 1760, and Thomas Craft of Bow has left record of the fact that he had a bowl 'burned in Mr. Gyles' Kiln' at a cost of 3s. in that year.

Birds having an 'agitated' appearance were quite commonly done at this studio, and the painter was wittily named, by the late W. B. Honey, 'The Master of the Dishevelled Birds.'

Although Worcester appear to have supplied Giles willingly enough in the early days, they later found it more profitable to decorate their products at the factory, and, like Duesbury before him, Giles found white porcelain progressively more difficult to get. No doubt this accounts for specimens decorated with an opaque green ground, for instance, in which sparse factory decoration can be traced underneath if they are held to the light. No doubt, too, it accounts for specimens of transfer printing colored over with enamels. A sale catalogue of Worcester porcelain of 1769 records a 'compleat tea and coffee equipage with handles jet enameled (transfer printed) *L'Amour* (a Hancock print), forty-three pieces. Bought by Mr. Giles.'

An examination of the work which can reasonably be attributed to Giles shows that he did many of the things decorated with colored grounds which form a much-prized group of Worcester porcelain, and the late H. R. Marshall, some of whose superb collection of Worcester is illustrated here, was of the opinion, after examining surviving records, that Giles decorated an enormous quantity of porcelain from this factory during the decade 1760–1770, a verdict with which the present writer entirely concurs. The quality, too, was fully equal to the work done by the factory, when, indeed, it did not surpass it. An adequate indication of this is provided by Plate 150, which is one of four plates presented to the Victoria and Albert Museum by a descendant of James Giles, Mrs. Dora Grubbe. There is a family tradition that it was decorated for the wedding of Mary Giles, daughter of James Giles.

The style of the Giles workshop can also be traced on some Chelsea porcelain of the gold anchor period, an interesting group being painted in green monochrome over black outlines. These must, undoubtedly, be attributed to an outside decorator, because specimens of white Chinese porcelain similarly decorated in England are known. Some of these are strongly reminiscent of the work of Jeffryes Hamett O'Neale, the Irish miniature painter previously mentioned in considering the work of

Chelsea, and his signature sometimes appears on more elaborate vases and plates, usually with animal subjects in conjunction with a dark blue ground (see Plate 146). John Donaldson, a Scottish miniaturist who painted some of the finer Worcester vases about the same time, no doubt worked outside the factory, and an example of his work appears on Plate 152.

By 1770 the factory appears to have been fully capable of doing all the more elaborate kinds of decoration previously done by Giles, we find many adaptations from Sèvres styles, and a number of important services were made for highly-placed customers which can be identified.

Few figures were made at Worcester, and these not until about 1769. Specimens are illustrated on Plates 153 and 166. All of those at present known appear to have been modeled by Mr. Tebo. It is by no means certain that everything thus made has been identified, and a number of discoveries in this field have been made within recent years.

Until 1772 the Holdships seem to have been the moving spirits at Worcester, and after Richard Holdship left in 1759, Josiah appears to have been almost solely responsible. In 1772, however, the factory was bought by the Reverend Thomas Vernon for £5.250, and then transferred to a Company headed by Dr. John Wall. By this means, all the original shareholders were eliminated, except Wall and Davis. Dr. Wall died in 1776, and the factory was sold to a new owner, Thomas Flight a merchant who had formerly been its London agent, in 1783. Until recently the period between 1751 and 1783 has been known as the 'Wall period,' on the assumption that John Wall was mainly responsible for its development. Recent research and fresh evaluation of the evidence, however, has led to the inescapable conclusion that Wall did not play a leading part until 1772. It would, therefore, be strictly in accord with the facts to describe the period from 1752 to 1772 as the 'Holdship period,' reserving the term 'Wall period' for the years from 1772 onwards. By a convenient fiction the period can well be extended to 1783, since the factory's products did not undergo any notable changes in style until this year.

The Flight family made a number of alterations in the body, and adopted, to some extent, the neo-classical style. Topographical landscape painting of considerable merit appears on some vases of the period. A number of things – the scale-blue ground with exotic birds in panels, for instance – continued to be made. Figures were discontinued with the departure of Tebo for Bristol, and the later production is almost entirely devoted to services and vases. In 1792, Robert Chamberlain opened another factory in Worcester, which eventually absorbed the earlier establishment.

The Worcester use of soaprock in porcelain was an innovation later copied in Liverpool at a factory opened in 1756 by Richard Chaffers with the assistance of Robert Podmore, who was at the original Bristol factory. They made a number of things of excellent quality in the early Worcester style, which are sometimes confused with the work of the latter factory. At Caughley, in Shropshire, a factory for the manufacture of useful wares was established by Thomas Turner in 1772, who was joined by Hancock in 1774. They made much ware decorated with blue transfer prints. Occasional specimens painted with enamel colors were probably done by Humphrey Chamberlain, son of Robert Chamberlain, who functioned as an independent decorator.

Worcester porcelain is an especial favorite with collectors. It has survived in considerable quantities, it is always well made and in good taste, and it is not difficult to identify. There are few things which, from an esthetic standpoint, are important in the way that some Chelsea wares are important, but there is also nothing to match the occasional Chelsea lapses into overdecorated vulgarity which occur during the gold anchor period.

LONGTON HALL (STAFFORDSHIRE)

UNTIL RECENTLY almost nothing was known of this factory, and attributions were made by a process of elimination based on a few newspaper advertisements. Since the recent discoveries by Dr. Bernard Watney, however, it is probably the best-documented of all English undertakings.

Ownership was formerly assigned to William Littler, a salt-glaze potter who started life at Brownhills, near Burslem. It has now become evident that he was a partner only, at first with William Jenkinson and William Nicklin, and that Jenkinson had obtained the 'Art Secret or Mystery' of porcelain making from elsewhere. It is also evident that Jenkinson had established a small factory before becoming a partner in the Longton Hall enterprise, which commenced in 1750. There is reason to believe that Jenkinson had some connection with the defunct Limehouse factory previously mentioned in discussing the early wares of Bristol. Watney suggests, very reasonably, that Jenkinson may, in fact, have been one of the principals at Limehouse, and the connection of Duesbury of Derby with the factory at a later date, although nebulous, is proved by mention of his name in a schedule attached to one of the factory agreements, which refers to money owing to 'Mr. Duesbury,' perhaps for enameling.

In 1755 Jenkinson sold his interest in the factory to Nathaniel Firmin, a gilder, and Robert Charlesworth also became a partner, as well as principal financial backer. Firmin died and left his share to his son, Samuel Firmin, and on the 23rd May, 1760, we find the following advertisement in *Aris's Birmingham Gazette*:

'All persons are hereby desired to take Notice, that the partnership between Mr. William Littler and Company, of Longton Hall aforesaid, and Mr. Robert Charlesworth, is dissolved, pursuant to their Articles and Agreements, and that they are to give no Credit to the said William Littler & Company, on account of the said Robert Charlesworth.'

This was followed by an advertisement on the 30th June, inserted by William Littler & Company:

'...William Littler & Company think proper to acquaint the Publick that it's not in Robert Charlesworth's Power to dissolve the Partnership therein mentioned, without consent of the rest of the Partners; that the said William Littler & Co. are far from the Expectation of any Credit on the said Charlesworth's account, and are all very desirous to execute any proper instrument for the Dissolution of the said Partnership, on having fair Accounts settled, and Damages paid by the said Charlesworth for his many Breaches of Covenant, and his late unjustifiable and illegal, tho' impotent and ineffectual, Attempt to put a Stop to the said Manufactory.'

Evidently the relationship had become extremely acrimonious, and on the 8th September, 1760, an advertisement signed by Samuel Firmin marks the end:

'...lest it should be insinuated or apprehended that I have at present any Concern in carrying on the said Works, I hereby declare, that I esteem the Partnership therein as dissolved on the 23rd May last, pursuant to the notice sent me by Mr. Robert Charlesworth.'

The date for the beginning of Jenkinson's manufacture was probably 1749, and to this period belong some white figures with a thick, lustrous, glassy glaze which, for this reason, are called 'Snowman' figures. The existing models are often derived from other sources – from Staffordshire salt-glazed and lead-glazed pottery, from Chelsea, and from Meissen. These were followed by some primitive wares decorated in underglaze blue. The following years show progressive refinements in body, in form, and in decoration, and some exceptional painting done by a topographical artist, often referred to as the 'Castle Painter' (Plate 174), is among the factory's most distinguished work. He was possibly John Hayfield, who is mentioned in the documents as being the only painter employed by the factory at the time.

Much work, too, was done in the form of leaves (Plate 154). These wares are mentioned in an advertisement in the *London Public Advertiser* in 1757:

'A New and curious Porcelain or China of the Longton Hall Manufactory, which has the Approbation of the best Judges, and recommended by several of the Nobility to this public Method of Sale. Consisting of Tureens, Covers and Dishes, large Cups and Covers, Jars and Beakers, with beautiful sprigs of flowers, open work'd Fruit Baskets and Plates, Variety of Services for Deserts, Tea and Coffee Equipages, Sauce Boats, leaf Basons and Plates, Melons, Colliflowers, elegant Epargnes (center-pieces) and other ornamental and useful Porcelain, both white and enamell'd'
whilst another advertisement in *Aris's Birmingham Gazette* two months later mentions:

'... Leaf-Plates, Sauce-Boats, and Variety of curious useful ornaments for Deserts, with Figures and Flowers of all Sorts, made exactly to Nature, allow'd by the best Judges to be the finest in England, where all Gentlemen and Ladies who please to honour him with their Commands may depend upon having the Favour greatly acknowledg'd and all Tradesmen who favour him with Orders, may depend upon having them faithfully executed by their most obedient humble Servant William Littler.'

This is a refreshing antidote to the blatant vulgarity of modern advertising, and even the claim that the 'best Judges' allowed it to be the finest in England is at least a dignified prevarication.

Some of the plainer wares were decorated with excellent bird painting in a characteristic palette, whilst flower sprays were well painted by an unknown artist, often referred to as the 'Trembly Rose' painter.

The factory made many figures which are not always well-finished, but are esthetically very pleasing, and much sought by collectors. Some of them are copied from Italian bronzes and small sculpture. A figure of Hercules slaying the Nemean Lion by tearing its jaws apart, for instance, is based on a boxwood carving by Stefano Maderno, and a *putto* mounted on a horse, which is in the British Museum, is similarly based on a 17th century Italian bronze. The superb figure of the Duke of Brunswick here illustrated (Plate 177) is shown mounted on a Lipizaner horse from the Spanish

Riding School of Vienna, and is an obvious derivation from a Meissen model, but it has lost nothing by its translation. The horse is in a typical Lipizaner pose, and trained horses from this source were supplied to the German nobility. Such derivations from Meissen are not unusual, but the quality is rarely so good.

There were, too, many figures taken from native sources, especially such *genre* figures as a pair of *Cooks*, a *Butter-seller*, and the like. Among the later figure productions may be numbered a pair of *Musicians*, and a group of *Dancers*, as well as a pair representing *Liberty and Matrimony*, a favorite subject. This class have passages of an unusual reddish-brown opaque pigment which is quite distinctive. A salt-glazed version of the *Musicians* is known, and an earlier pair of a *Turk and Companion* is also known in salt glaze, perhaps enameled by Duesbury.

Two remarkable figures illustrated by Watney (*Longton Hall Porcelain* – Plate 61a and b) deserve mention. These, representing *Spring* and *Autumn*, are on characteristic *rococo* scroll bases. Watney gives them a date between 1753 and 1757, and, from the center, rises a background of *rococo* scrolls extremely similar to those to be seen from Nymphenburg on such Bustelli models as the *Turkish Lady and Gentleman at Coffee*, done in 1760. It is surprising to find that this particular development of the *rococo* style reached provincial England so quickly.

Mention should be made of 'Littler's blue' – a rich, streaky, blue ground which appears alike on porcelain and on rare specimens of salt-glazed ware. It is found with overpainting of white enamel, and with oil gilding.

The influence of the *rococo* style is to be seen in some small vases, often a little lopsided in appearance, which, when the covers have survived, are surmounted by bouquets of modeled flowers obviously derived ultimately from the mid-century fashion for them at Vincennes. In some rare instances, these vases reach a large size, and are sometimes surmounted by birds and figures among the flowers.

Generally, despite its derivations, the porcelain of Longton Hall is unsophisticated and entirely English in feeling. Perhaps, for this reason, it is an especial favorite with collectors who subscribe to the peculiarly English cult of 'amateurism' – a kind of harmless inverted snobbery which despises the greater polish and sophistication of the professional. At its best the work of this factory has a great deal of provincial charm which is unusually pleasing.

LOWESTOFT (SUFFOLK)

THIS FACTORY was the subject of a ludicrous error by William Chaffers, author of *Marks and Monograms on Pottery and Porcelain*, who attributed to it the large amount of surviving Chinese export porcelain decorated with Armorial bearings. In consequence, this is still known in some quarters as 'Oriental Lowestoft.' There is, of course, no connection whatever between the two.

In 1756 Hewlin Luson, a Suffolk landowner, discovered clay on his estate. He brought workmen from London, and tried to start a factory, but a London competitor bribed his men to spoil the work, and the attempt was given up. A Company was formed in 1757 under the managership of Robert Browne, and it is said that he hid in a barrel in the Bow factory to observe the mixing of the body. It seems certain that some information was gained from Bow, because the Lowestoft body is almost exactly the same, containing a comparable quantity of bone ash.

Differentiation between porcelain painted in blue from Lowestoft and Bow is difficult, but the Lowestoft blue has often run, or has been smeared. The glaze is usually thicker than that used at Bow, and has a pronounced greenish tone, as well as being full of minute bubbles. Most such printed wares come from Lowestoft, examples of blue printing at Bow being negligible in quantity.

In 1902 excavations were carried out in premises owned by a firm of brewers, Messrs. Morse, in Crown Street, Lowestoft, and plaster molds and other fragments were brought to light. From these it has been possible to identify some naive figures, although examples are extremely scarce.

An additional aid to attribution is formed by a number of inscribed wares – mugs and so forth – of which 'A Trifle from Lowestoft' is typical. Birth tablets, too, are sometimes to be seen. These, made for commemorative purposes, are inscribed with the name and date of birth of the child.

Enameled wares are often copies of Chinese 'Mandarin' patterns, and the palette includes a characteristic mauve pink or carmine.

Much Lowestoft porcelain was made in imitation of the work of other English factories, and specimens with the crescent or script 'W' marks of Worcester are not uncommon. The crossed swords of Meissen, too, are to be seen on a few specimens.

The work of this factory is represented here by Plate 179 and 180, two rare subjects which are peculiarly English. Plate 179 proves that a devotion to the game of cricket is by no means a modern weakness, whilst Plate 180 illustrates the craft of shipbuilding which was carried on in the port of Lowestoft.

CHINESE PORCELAIN probably came first to Europe in the 14th century. One of the most tantalizing of surviving records is that of a Chinese vase mounted in silver with the Arms of Louis the Great of Hungary (1342–1382), which was bought from the Royal Collections of France at the end of the 18th century by William Beckford, the eccentric author of *Vathek*. This, known from drawings, appeared in the Fonthill Abbey sale of 1822, and has since completely vanished. Other examples still exist which can be dated both from the porcelain itself, and from the European silver mounts. Such things were treasured, and mounting in silver was commonly practiced.

This translucent substance, porcelain, from a fabulous land, was so rare that the secret of making it was earnestly sought by European potters for centuries. The problem was ultimately solved in two distinct ways. Towards the end of the 16th century a kind of porcelain was made in Florence (Medici porcelain) which was fundamentally clay and ground glass. It had the desired quality of translucency, but was softer than the true Chinese porcelain. This 'soft' porcelain was later extensively manufactured in France – at St. Cloud, Mennecy, Vincennes-Sèvres, and elsewhere – and, later still, in England. Nevertheless, some potters did not lose sight of the fact that it was only a substitute, and porcelain in the Chinese manner was first made in Europe by Ehrenfried Walther von Tschirnhaus, a member of the Saxon Court, who provided the formula used by the Meissen factory. In England, William Cookworthy, a Quaker chemist of Plymouth, also searched for the secret.

He first appears in our story in 1745, when he discussed Virginian china clay with Duché. He did not, however, make use of this discovery, and later found both the essential ingredients of true porcelain on the estate of Lord Camelford about 1754. Tradition has it that his horse slipped, and turned up white clay with its hoof, but the same story is told of Johann Schnorr von Carolsfeld at Meissen, and it is, therefore, probably no more than a fable.

Chinese porcelain is composed of clay which, being refractory, retains its shape during firing, and a feldspathic rock which vitrifies like glass and is extremely hard. No doubt Cookworthy realized this, and it is, at least, possible that his first attempts to find the vitrifiable part of the Chinese secret led him to soaprock. This behaves in much the same way under heat, but is softer than the feldspathic rock ultimately used. The possibility that he supplied the information which led to the establishment of the early Bristol factory already discussed is, therefore, one to be reckoned with.

By 1765 Cookworthy had succeeded in making a true porcelain, and he established a factory for its manufacture on a commercial scale at Plymouth in 1768. The earliest specimens are distinctly primitive. Both smoke staining and fire cracks are common faults.

The Plymouth factory opened at a time when most other factories were financially in low water. It is, for this reason, possible that Mr. Tebo, the modeler already discussed, made his way to Plymouth before going on to Worcester in 1769. This inference can fairly be drawn from the number of Plymouth models which strongly resemble the work of Bow. Prominent among them are some shell-salts resembling those from Bow, which were often marked T° and made there about twenty years earlier, as well as figures of lions, some of which are identical with Bow models. Another problem, too, is presented by some busts of George II, perhaps from a portrait by Roubiliac at Windsor Castle. I have closely examined one example recently, and this appeared to be of true porcelain similar to that made by Cookworthy, and therefore accords with the tradition that a bust of this kind was made at the factory, and was one of the family heirlooms. Others exist which are probably of Chelsea manufacture, and most have been thus attributed by various authorities.

Models closely resembling those of Longton Hall exist. One or two have such slight alterations as could be made by the 'repairer'. This man put figures together from the molded components, and could make minor changes in so doing. In this way, a pair of *Cooks* from Longton Hall become *Musicians* at Plymouth by the simple expedient of changing their cooking pots for musical instruments and making slight alterations to the base. In other ways, they remain the same. The Longton Hall group of two boys feeding grapes to a goat (Plate 176) also appears in a Plymouth version almost unaltered. These resemblances cannot be explained as an example of interfactory copying. They are too exact. Neither can they be regarded as the result of the use of a common source of inspiration, and the conclusion that Cookworthy acquired molds from these factories seems inescapable. Those from Longton Hall were no doubt sold when the factory closed. It is possible that some molds could have been acquired from Chelsea in 1768 when the factory was for sale, which may account for the portrait of George II, whilst those from Bow were probably brought by someone from the factory. Who else but Mr. Tebo?

Most surviving Plymouth wares were intended for useful purposes rather than for decoration. Some excellent bird painting has been attributed to a M. Soqui, said to have come from Sèvres, who may have been responsible, later, for bird painting at Worcester in the manner of the Sèvres artists, Evans and Aloncle. Some rare specimens have been noticed which were painted by James Giles in London, one of which bears a Chelsea gold anchor. Armorial bearings appear on some things, and were, no doubt, copies of Chinese export porcelain of this kind, whilst tea and coffee pots often resemble those of Worcester in form. Cups and saucers are rare, but it is possible to see a spiral 'wreathing' in the body, whilst cup handles are often slightly askew – a peculiarity to be seen in later porcelain from Bristol.

Cookworthy was primarily a chemist. On the Continent he would have been called an arcanist – one who had the *arcanum* or secret of porcelain making. His artistic gifts appear to have been small, and there was, no doubt, too little money available with which to employ artists of talent. His work, therefore, leaned heavily on that of other factories in its more decorative aspects.

In 1770 Cookworthy transferred the factory to Castle Green in Bristol, and, two years later, he gave a licence to Richard Champion to use the patent. The patent was transferred to Champion in 1774, and soon after this assignment Champion petitioned the House of Commons for the extension of the rights conferred for a further period of fourteen years. Despite opposition from Josiah Wedgwood, this was successful. Champion may have got his interest in porcelain manufacture from his brother-in-law in South Carolina, who sent him a supply of *unaker* for experimental purposes. Probably he and Cookworthy met each other in 1765, when it appears that some experiments in porcelain making were made in Bristol by the latter. Champion refers to a factory 'set up here some time ago on the principle of the Chinese porcelain, but not being successful is given up.'

Considerable differences in the style of manufacture were introduced at once by Champion, and the new factory had much greater command of the material. The styles are, for the most part, those of Meissen and Sèvres, with occasional excursions into derivations from Chinese porcelain. Plates obviously gave difficulty, and some have a double foot ring to prevent sagging and warping. Some interesting plaques were made in *biscuit*, decorated with modeled flowers, perhaps by Thomas Briand, who has already been mentioned in connection with the Chelsea factory. A number of special services were made for particular customers.

Some excellent figures were made, some perhaps supplied by Stephan, formerly of Derby, and by John Bacon, R.A., who is known to have done work of the kind for Duesbury and Wedgwood. The influence of Derby is noticeable. Tebo appears to have modeled no figures for this factory, but his sign appears on a number of things, including several figures, where he seems to have functioned only as a 'repairer.' A figure of *Winter* from a set of the Seasons is known with the T^o mark impressed, and it is possible to see in it some of the characteristics noticeable in his earlier work, although the original inspiration is obviously not his.

By 1778 Champion was in financial difficulties, and he attempted to sell the factory. Little work was done thereafter, and the *Bristol Journal* for April, 1782, carried the following advertisement:

'To be sold by Hand, on Monday, the 29th instant, at the late Manufactory at Castle Green, the remaining stock of Enamels, blue and white, and white Bristol China. The manufactory being removed to the North.'

The patent was sold to a company of potters who opened a small factory at New Hall in Staffordshire, where useful wares were made. Champion emigrated to South Carolina in 1784, and died in 1791.

Early in the 19th century New Hall changed to the standard English bone china body, and no serious attempts have been made to make true porcelain in England since, although it is the preferred body elsewhere.

146. PLATE. WORCESTER PORCELAIN. C. 1765

18.5 cm. Collection: Major-General Sir Harold Wernher, Bart., Luton Hoo, Bedfordshire

This plate has a *gros bleu* ground, and the center is surrounded by diaper ornament in gold which is the Worcester version of the *rococo*. The painting is by Jeffryes Hamett O'Neale, and shows him at his most lighthearted. It illustrates the Fable of the Bear and the Honey (see Plates 87 and 147).

---

147. DISH. WORCESTER PORCELAIN. C. 1765

Diameter 30 cm. The Ashmolean Museum of Fine Art (H. R. Marshall Collection), Oxford

A large dish with wavy rim, scale-blue ground, and rich gilding. The center panel is derived from the illustration to Fable LXXXI of Aesop by Francis Barlow, and is characteristic of the later work of Jeffryes Hamett O'Neale. The panels of horses and cattle are also by the hand of O'Neale, but the birds may be by another artist. O'Neale's light and amusing touch is well seen in this dish, which should be compared with Plate 146, and his much earlier work in the same vein at Chelsea (Plate 87).

---

148. VASE. WORCESTER PORCELAIN. C. 1765

28.5 cm. The Ashmolean Museum of Fine Art (H. R. Marshall Collection), Oxford

A hexagonal vase with scale-blue ground and rich gilding, painted with a rare *chinoiserie* subject after Pillement. This appears to have been the work of the Giles studio, since a Chelsea service is similarly decorated, and Giles is known to have painted white porcelain from both factories. The style bears a certain resemblance to the so-called 'Chinese Chippendale' of English furniture, and this vase may have been made for such a decorative scheme.

---

149. COFFEEPOT. WORCESTER PORCELAIN. C. 1765

23.4 cm. Collection: Major-General Sir Harold Wernher, Bart., Luton Hoo, Bedfordshire

An example of the Worcester scale-ground. The use of this particular color is exceptional. Most scale-grounds were carried out in underglaze blue, and were executed fairly meticulously on the early examples, but much more sketchily later. This is not, however, a certain way of estimating the date, since some running and smudging was almost unavoidable with underglaze blue. Examples decorated in overglaze colors in this way are always of the highest quality, and some are attributable to James Giles. They are among the rarest of all specimens of Worcester porcelain.

150. PLATE. WORCESTER PORCELAIN. C. 1765

22.5 cm. The Victoria and Albert Museum, London

This plate, superbly decorated with game birds, was presented to the Museum by Mrs. Dora Grubbe, a descendant of James Giles, the decorator, of Clerkenwell (see page 209). For this reason this specimen is documentary, since it is undoubtedly the work of Giles, and can therefore be used to attribute other work. The dead fox on the ledge of the plate at the left suggests the hand of O'Neale, and the possibility of a connection between the two men is a reasonable supposition.

---

151. DESSERT BASKET. WORCESTER PORCELAIN. C. 1770

Height (basket) 13.5 cm. Width (dish) 27 cm.
The Ashmolean Museum of Fine Art (H. R. Marshall Collection), Oxford

A dessert basket of quatrefoil form with twig handles, the cover pierced with an openwork trellis pattern. These baskets, derived from Meissen, were very popular at the time. The example shown has unusual cornucopia-shaped passages of claret enamel almost overlaid with rich gilt ornament. The same motif appears inside the basket, on the bottom.

---

152. VASE. WORCESTER PORCELAIN. C. 1770

54 cm. Collection: Major-General Sir Harold Wernher, Bart., Luton Hoo, Bedfordshire

This baluster vase has a *gros bleu* ground derived from Vincennes, and the large center panel is painted by the Scottish miniaturist, John Donaldson. It bears his initials, JD. On the reverse is a panel of superbly painted flowers, whilst the panels on the cover are painted by O'Neale, the obelisk bearing an inscription in a cryptic language peculiar to this painter. Donaldson, whose work is highly valued, came to London from Scotland about 1759, and was a member (with O'Neale) of the Incorporated Society of Artists.

---

153. SPORTSMAN AND COMPANION. WORCESTER PORCELAIN
C. 1770

18.5 cm. The Ashmolean Museum of Fine Art (H. R. Marshall Collection), Oxford

The man holds a flintlock sporting gun, the woman a powder flask and a dead bird. Few figures were made at Worcester, and almost all of the known models were done by Mr. Tebo. For many years it was thought that no figures were made here, but a contemporary reference in the diary of Mrs. Philip Lybbe Powys mentions seeing them made during a visit to the factory. The first specimens were definitely identified by the late William King in 1923. This attribution has since been confirmed by chemical analyses. Specimens are extremely rare.

146

147

148

149

151

153

154

155

154. TUREEN. LONGTON HALL PORCELAIN. C. 1756

Height 15.5 cm. The Victoria and Albert Museum (Schreiber Collection), London

This tureen, representing a melon, is on a leaf-shaped stand. It is typical of the work of this factory, where leaf forms of all kinds found especial favor. Tureens of varying size in the form of the lettuce, the cabbage, the cauliflower, and so forth were made at Chelsea, and a Worcester cauliflower tureen appears on Plate 165.

---

155. FIGURE OF AN ACTOR. LONGTON HALL PORCELAIN C. 1758

19.5 cm. The Victoria and Albert Museum (Schreiber Collection), London

This figure is said to represent the actor, David Garrick, and of its connection with the stage there can be no doubt. Apart from the theatrical mask on the front of the pedestal, the book is inscribed:

> The cloud cap . . . . .
> The gorgeous . . . . .

The remainder is illegible, but the missing words are easy to supply:

> 'The cloud capp'd towers, the gorgeous palaces,
> The solemn temples, the great globe itself'

– part of Prospero's speech from the fourth act of Shakespeare's *Tempest*.

David Garrick (1717–1799) is generally regarded as the greatest actor of the 18th century. He frequently appeared in Shakespeare's plays.

---

156. PHOENIX AMID FLAMES. PLYMOUTH PORCELAIN. C. 1770

20 cm. Collection: Major-General Sir Harold Wernher, Bart., Luton Hoo, Bedfordshire

These much resemble certain Bow models in their characteristics. The bases, for instance, are not unlike those used at Bow, whilst the birds strongly resemble that on which Zeus is mounted (Plate 132). The same kind of bird appears as a vase finial at Worcester (Plate 170). They are almost certainly all by the hand of the Bow modeler, Mr. Tebo.

---

157. VASE. LUND'S BRISTOL PORCELAIN. C. 1750

27 cm. The Syndics of the Fitzwilliam Museum, Cambridge

This hexagonal vase comes from the parent factory of the Worcester undertaking. The Chinese subject is delicately penciled, and painted in a palette which includes a *rose* enamel derived from the *famille rose* porcelain of the Emperors, Yung Chêng and Ch'ien Lung. The size of the vase, as well as the quality of the decoration, proves that manufacture was well developed before the transference of the factory to Worcester.

160

161

163

164

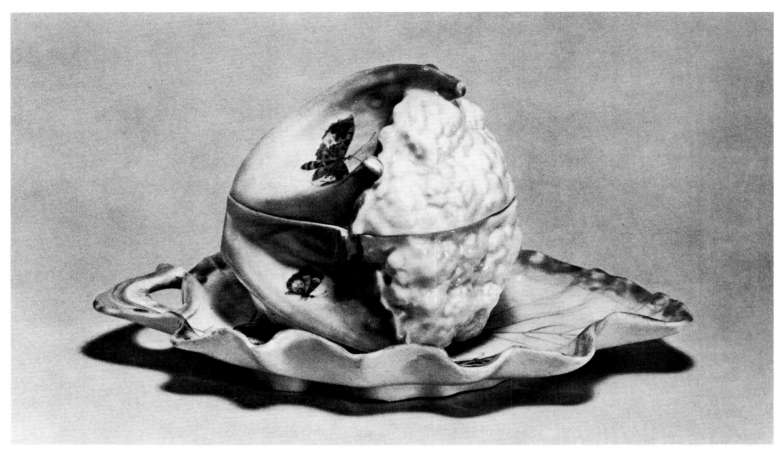

165

168

169

170

171

175

176

179

180

184

158. SAUCEBOAT. BRISTOL-WORCESTER PORCELAIN. C. 1752

18.5 cm. The Victoria and Albert Museum (Gift: E. F. Broderip), London

This sauceboat is either among the last things to be made at Lund's Bristol factory, or among the first to come from Worcester. It is of a pronounced silver pattern, and the molded swags of flowers are colored with enamels. The snake handle is typical of some silver handles of the period. Under the base the word 'Bristoll' has been molded, and covered with a leaf colored in green enamel, probably to obliterate it. If, therefore, it was made at Worcester, the mold for it was brought from Bristol at the time of the transfer. See page 207.

159. MUG. WORCESTER PORCELAIN. C. 1752

15 cm. The Ashmolean Museum of Fine Art (H. R. Marshall Collection), Oxford

This mug has a spreading foot and a grooved strap handle. The decoration is in underglaze blue, touched over with linear detail in iron-red, recalling the Chinese combination of underglaze blue and copper red in use from early Ming times. The subject is derived from Chinese porcelain, and represents a fisherman in a river landscape, with willows, bamboos, and pines. It is characteristic of early Worcester porcelain, at which time decoration was almost entirely dependent on Chinese sources.

160. DISH. WORCESTER PORCELAIN. C. 1765

24.5 cm. The Ashmolean Museum of Fine Art (H. R. Marshall Collection), Oxford

This hexagonal dish is an exact copy of a Chinese prototype of the early part of the 18th century. It has a seeded border in *famille verte* enamel. The phoenix (*fêng huang*) in the center has a green back and blue wings. The tree is aubergine, the table yellow. The outer gadrooned border is orange-red and gold. Worcester was much more influenced in its work by Chinese porcelain than the other English porcelain factories.

161. DISH. WORCESTER PORCELAIN. C. 1765

Greatest width 47.5 cm.
The Victoria and Albert Museum (Schreiber Collection), London

This oval dish has a molded border of flowers and shell forms, as well as a bird, a lizard, and fish, amid *rococo* scrolls. The molded ornament is colored with puce, yellow, and green enamels, and the center is decorated with three transfers printed in black. The left-hand print shows Trajan's Column in the background, and was apparently taken from an Italian topographical engraving. The three prints are from separate plates, and do not appear to be related. Lady Charlotte Schreiber bought this dish in London in 1884, when, no doubt misled by the unusual border, she thought it to be Bow.

162. LEAF DISH. WORCESTER PORCELAIN. C. 1765

35.5 cm. The Ashmolean Museum of Fine Art (H. R. Marshall Collection), Oxford

The dish, in the form of two overlapping leaves, has molded veins, the two main ribs being touched lightly with puce. The flower sprays are in puce, whilst the landscape is painted with orange-red, copper green, and yellow, with mauve hills.

163. VASE. WORCESTER PORCELAIN. C. 1765

15 cm. The Ashmolean Museum of Fine Art (H. R. Marshall Collection), Oxford

Beaker-shaped vase depicting a coy lady and a sprightly gallant amusingly painted with yellow, purple, green, and orange-red enamels by Jeffryes Hamett O'Neale. This is an unusual subject for O'Neale, and was no doubt done for a special purpose.

164. WALL POCKET. WORCESTER PORCELAIN. C. 1765

25.5 cm. The Ashmolean Museum of Fine Art (H. R. Marshall Collection), Oxford

This molded wall pocket, or cornucopia, is pierced for suspension. The flowers in relief at the top are colored in puce, yellow, green, and blue enamels. The flowers lower down are derived from the Meissen *indianische Blumen* (India flowers). The metalwork origin of this specimen can especially be seen in the molded tip to the horn.

165. TUREEN AND STAND. WORCESTER PORCELAIN. C. 1765

12.5 cm. The Ashmolean Museum of Fine Art (H. R. Marshall Collection), Oxford

Tureens in this form, comparatively frequent at Chelsea and Longton Hall, are very rare from Worcester. The leaf-shaped stand is edged with green, and the veins are indicated in puce. The cauliflower is green, shading to yellow at the base. All parts are transfer printed with moths, an embellishment not be seen from either of the other two factories mentioned.

166. GARDENER AND COMPANION. WORCESTER PORCELAIN C. 1770

16.5 cm. Collection: Irwin Untermyer, Esq., New York

The gardener wears a black hat, pale yellow coat trimmed with rose, a blue apron, and breeches striped with puce, yellow, red, and green. His companion wears a yellow hat with a red ribbon, a rose-colored gown with blue cuffs, a flowered white apron, and a puce ribbon at her neck. The figures are unmarked.

These very rare figures were the first to be identified as coming from Worcester by the late William King of the British Museum. There is a noticeable resemblance in the style of the modeling to those shown in Plate 153, and also to some of the Bow figures of 1760. There is little doubt that they were modeled by the ubiquitous Mr. Tebo, and some examples are known which bear the impressed mark assigned to him.

There is, equally, no doubt of their Worcester origin. Comparable figures have been analyzed chemically, and the result has not differed noticeably in the percentage of magnesium oxide (a major constituent of soaprock) from Worcester service ware. An interesting complication of the position may be found in a few known examples of Bow figures which bear the crescent mark of Worcester. These, on analysis, prove to be indistinguishable from other Bow figures, and there can be no doubt of their Bow origin. Worcester figures never bear any of the recognized factory marks.

---

167. VASE OF HEXAGONAL FORM. WORCESTER PORCELAIN
C. 1770

42.5 cm. Collection: Irwin Untermyer, Esq., New York

This vase has a blue scale ground, with diaper patterns and scrollwork in gold. The panels are painted by the Irish miniaturist, Jeffryes Hamett O'Neale, whose work is represented also on Plates 146 and 163. The scenes are from the *Commedia dell'Arte* – the Italian Comedy – which enjoyed enormous popularity on the Continent, and was a frequent subject for porcelain decoration and the modeling of figures.

The Comedy itself is of great antiquity, being directly linked with the popular theatrical entertainments of Greek and Roman times. It became extremely popular during the 16th century, and was, perhaps, revived by Francesco Cherea, leading player to Pope Leo x. It existed only in the form of a *scenario*, the dialogue and the stage 'business' being improvized by the players.

The Italian Comedy was, as the name suggests, a lighthearted production dealing with amorous intrigues and amusing rogueries. O'Neale was at his best in the witty delineation of both human and animal figures, and here we see the humorous vein in which he excelled.

The vase is one of a set of three and was exhibited in 'Masterpieces of European Porcelain at the Metropolitan Museum of New York in 1949.

---

168. SUGAR BOWL. WORCESTER PORCELAIN. C. 1765

13.5 cm. Collection: W. R. B. Young, Esq., St. Leonards-on-Sea, Sussex

This example, a common Worcester shape, has a sponged blue ground (*gros bleu*), instead of the more usual scale-blue. The same shape is found with transfer printing, and other kinds of decoration. The exotic birds are typical of a large number of specimens, and there is a slight glaze retraction inside the foot ring – almost invariable at this time. The gilding is well executed, but is thinner than that to be seen on Chelsea of the gold anchor period, and usually has a slightly brown tinge. The bird painting was probably done in the studio of James Giles, and 'blanks' – that is, pieces decorated with a *gros bleu* or scale-blue ground, but without either painting or gilding in the reserves – can sometimes be seen. These are in the form in which they were supplied to Giles for painting.

169. DESSERT BASKET. WORCESTER PORCELAIN. C. 1769

16 cm. Ashmolean Museum of Fine Art (H. R. Marshall Collection), Oxford

Openwork baskets were a specialty of the Worcester factory, although they were made else-where, notably at Derby. The set of small baskets with applied flowers in this style, however, are peculiar to Worcester, and they are referred to in a sale catalogue of 1769 as 'A stand, with pierced baskets.' The flowers are conventionally colored, and the base is an open triangle. Rosettes of small flowers are molded at the intersections. Baskets of this kind were a derivation from Meissen.

170. POTPOURRI VASE. WORCESTER PORCELAIN. C. 1770

28.5 cm. Ashmolean Museum of Fine Art (H. R. Marshall Collection), Oxford

Hexagonal vase ultimately derived from Meissen. The general form of this vase, with its applied 'frill' near the bottom, and the mask handles, was very popular, and can be seen from Bow and Derby with a circular section, and from Worcester and Bristol in hexagonal section. The Bow, Worcester, and Bristol examples were done by Mr. Tebo, and his mark appears on specimens from the two latter factories. The cover of this example is surmounted by an eagle, a rare feature, and the modeling should be compared with that of the bird son Plates 132 and 156, there attributed to the hand of Tebo. A much more usual knop to these vases is a simple flower, although a bird knop by another hand can be seen on some Derby vases. The *rococo* relief scrollwork is comparatively rare from Worcester, and suggests the hand of a modeler who did not work in the general tradition of the factory. A common variation has swags of modeled flowers in place of the scrolls. The example shown bears the impressed mark, *T⁰*, and the coloring is predominantly puce and green, with some yellow and iron-red.

171. STAND. WORCESTER PORCELAIN. C. 1775

30 cm. The Ashmolean Museum of Fine Art (H. R. Marshall Collection), Oxford

This dessert stand on a low foot is painted with exotic birds by an artist presumed to be M. Soqui referred to in discussing Plate 183, with which this should be compared. Much of the later bird painting from Worcester is by his hand. The foreground is of green and brown stripes, and the birds are painted with mauve, orange red, yellowish-green, and a 'dry' blue enamel characteristic of the Worcester palette.

172. MASK JUG. LIVERPOOL PORCELAIN. C. 1760

24.5 cm. The Victoria and Albert Museum (Schreiber Collection), London

This amusing jug is painted with a hunting scene in enamel colors. The hounds are in full cry after a hare. The top has a broad band of blue underglaze, decorated with gilding in a manner no doubt inspired by Sèvres. This jug was formerly attributed to Worcester, and it does resemble jugs from this factory lightly molded in the form of overlapping leaves, which have a similar mask on the pouring lip. The specimen illustrated is undoubtedly copied from this source, but lacks the molding. The handle is derived from silver. The body, like that of Worcester, contains a high percentage of soaprock.

173. WINTER. 'SNOWMAN' GROUP. LONGTON HALL PORCELAIN C. 1751

13 cm. The Syndics of the Fitzwilliam Museum, Cambridge

This figure probably represents Winter from a set of the Seasons, and depicts a child warming his hands in front of a stove. The illustration clearly shows the thick glassy glaze which is typical of this whole group (see page 213), and which has caused them to be dubbed 'Snowmen.' The flowers on the base are also characteristic.

174. TEAPOT. LONGTON HALL PORCELAIN. C. 1755

12 cm. The Victoria and Albert Museum (Schreiber Collection), London

This teapot is decorated with a French or Italian scene by the 'Castle Painter,' perhaps John Hayfield (page 213). Most surviving work of this kind appears to have been taken from Continental topographical engravings which were common enough in England at the time. The handle is in the form of a vine stem with grapes and leaves, and grapes form the knop. The spout has a frill of leaves on other side, a typical Longton Hall *motif*. The palette is the characteristic soft coloring of the factory.

175. TEAPOT. LONGTON HALL PORCELAIN. C. 1755

12 cm. The Trustees of the Cecil Higgins Museum, Bedford

This teapot is formed from overlapping cabbage leaves colored in green and yellow enamels, with puce veining. The stalk forms the handle. The form is characteristic of much Longton porcelain, and is mentioned in contemporary advertisements. An example of this kind in color is illustrated on Plate 154.

176. PUTTI WITH GOAT. LONGTON HALL PORCELAIN. C. 1758

14 cm. Trustees of the Cecil Higgins Museum, Bedford

One *putto* has yellow drapery, the other puce. The grapes are naturally colored, blackish-mauve with green leaves. The goat is flecked with mauve, and the scrolls of the base have been outlined with a similar color and touched with green. This group appears to be derived from an unidentified bronze. An almost identical version is to be seen from Plymouth some ten years later, and seems to be from the same molds.

177. THE DUKE OF BRUNSWICK. LONGTON HALL PORCELAIN
C. 1758

22 cm. The British Museum, London

Ferdinand, Duke of Brunswick (1721–1792), entered the Prussian service and commanded a regiment in the First and Second Silesian Wars. At the beginning of the Seven Years' War he commanded a division, and contributed to the Victory of Prague in 1757. He received the supreme command of Allied Forces from George II, and, during the next five years he successfully held at bay far more numerous forces by masterly strategy. On the 1st August, 1759, he gained a brilliant victory over Marshall Contades at Minden (see Plate 121). In 1766 he became estranged from Frederick the Great, who owed so much to his genius, and occupied his remaining years as a patron of art and learning. The superb portrait here shown appears to be derived from a Meissen model, and the Duke is shown mounted on a stallion from the Spanish Riding School at Vienna, which supplied trained horses to many of the ruling princes of central Europe. The pose is characteristic of these animals. The Duke wears a puce coat, and a light blue sash with a gold star.

---

178. PILGRIM. LONGTON HALL PORCELAIN. C. 1758

25 cm. The Trustees of the Cecil Higgins Museum, Bedford

This rare figure has the scallop shells of St. James at the shoulder. The model is by the same hand as a number of the later Longton figures, and he wears a rich yellow coat lined with puce which has green sleeves. The breeches are painted with a mauve enamel characteristic of the factory at this period. The base is washed with green. This has been a candlestick, but the nozzle is now missing.

---

179. JUG. LOWESTOFT PORCELAIN. C. 1765

17.5 cm. The Victoria and Albert Museum (Legh Tolson Bequest), London

This rare jug is worthy of inclusion if only because it illustrates an early form of the game of cricket, which has since almost assumed the status of a minor religious festival in English life. The game is thought to be Saxon in origin, but the first certain recorded mention seems to be in 1672, when a writer referred to 'morrice dancing, cudgel playing, crickets, and other sports.' When this jug was made cricket was a popular subject for wagers, large sums sometimes being staked on the result. The first written rules were drawn up in 1774. On the jug here shown the bat and wicket differ to some extent from those in use today. Decoration is in pale enamel colors, the field being indicated by brownish-green washes. On the other side the bowler and the rest of the fieldsmen are shown, and the diaper surround is painted in iron red. The jug is inscribed 'The Game of Cricket–Lowestoft,' and the design was taken from a print by H. Roberts after L. P. Boitard.

180. FLASK. LOWESTOFT PORCELAIN. C. 1765

14.5 cm. Collection: Geoffrey Godden, Esq., Worthing, Sussex

Lowestoft is a fishing port on the Suffolk coast, and shipbuilding was a local industry during the 18th century. This rare and interesting flask shows one such small ship under construction. The body much resembles that of Bow, and decoration is carried out in blue underglaze.

---

181. GARDENER AND COMPANION. PLYMOUTH PORCELAIN
C. 1770

Average height 23 cm. The Trustees of the Cecil Higgins Museum, Bedford

These figures are typically English in style, and the modeling of the woman in particular is reminiscent of some Staffordshire earthenware figures of the period. The man wears a coat painted with a light brownish-red, and the scrollwork on the base is touched with a similar color. This is fairly characteristic of Plymouth coloring. The style is unsophisticated, and the *rococo* bases were already a little unfashionable when these figures were made. The base strongly resembles some later Bow bases, made perhaps five years or so earlier. The hand is not that of Tebo, although the male figure resembles a gardener modeled by Tebo at Worcester, and the bases suggest his influence. The same models with minor variations are in the Victoria and Albert Museum.

---

182. MUG. CHAMPION'S BRISTOL PORCELAIN. C. 1775

16.5 cm. Collection: Major-General Sir Harold Wernher, Bart., Luton Hoo, Bedfordshire

A bell-shaped mug decorated with a diaper border of pink scales, and bouquets of flowers. It bears a black silhouette portrait of Richard Champion on a yellow ground within a laurel wreath. The initials, RC, are in gold.

---

183. VASE. CHAMPION'S BRISTOL PORCELAIN. C. 1775

39 cm. The Victoria and Albert Museum (Schreiber Collection), London

This vase, of hexagonal form, is magnificently decorated with exotic birds in the Sèvres style by a hand closely resembling that thought to be of M. Soqui. This artist, also referred to as Saqui and Lequoi, painted birds in the style of the Sèvres artists, Etienne Evans and François Aloncle, at Plymouth, Bristol, and Worcester. He is mentioned by Prideaux (*Relics of Wm. Cookworthy*) as an 'excellent painter and enameller from Sèvres.' The vase was bought by Lady Charlotte Schreiber in 1879 for £75 – a high price at the time (see Plate 171).

184. GOATHERD. CHAMPION'S BRISTOL PORCELAIN. C. 1775

28 cm. The Syndics of the Fitzwilliam Museum, Cambridge

This distinguished figure is dressed in a black hat, flowered waistcoat, yellow breeches, and brown belt and gaiters. He leans against a wooden fence. It is characteristic of the finest work of this factory. The *rococo* scrollwork has disappeared from the base under the influence of the neo-classical style. The figure is strongly influenced by Meissen figure modeling.

A companion figure is known bearing the impressed mark, T^o, but neither resembles the work of Mr. Tebo, and he must, therefore, have functioned only as a 'repairer.'

SELECTED BIBLIOGRAPHY

POTTERY

Burlington Fine Arts Club. Illustrated Catalogue of Early English Earthenware. London 1914.

Garner, F. H.: English Delftware. London 1948.

Honey, W. B.: Wedgwood Ware. London 1948.

Rackham, Bernard: Early Staffordshire Pottery. London 1948.

Rackham, Bernard: Medieval English Pottery. London 1945.

Rackham, Bernard and Read, H.: English Pottery. London 1924.

PORCELAIN

Barrett, F. A.: Worcester Porcelain. London 1953.

Eccles, Herbert and Rackham, Bernard: Analysed Specimens of English Porcelain. London 1922.

English Ceramic Circle. The commemorative catalogue of an Exhibition of English pottery and porcelain at the Victoria and Albert Museum. London 1952.

Honey, W. B.: Old English Porcelain. London 1948.

King, William: English Porcelain figures of the 18th century. London 1925.

King, William: Chelsea Porcelain. London 1922.

Savage, George: 18th century English Porcelain. London 1952.

Watney, Dr. Bernard: Longton Hall Porcelain. London 1957.

ENGLISH PORCELAIN

FACTORY MARKS

CHELSEA 1745–49. Incised. Known in underglaze blue

CHELSEA 1745. Incised

CHELSEA 1749. In underglaze blue

CHELSEA 1750–70. Raised on medallion, red, blue, lilac, brown and gold

CHELSEA-DERBY 1770–84. Red and gold

CHELSEA-DERBY 1770-1784. In gold

DERBY 1750. Incised

DERBY c. 1760. Incised

DERBY 1780–84. In blue or purple

DERBY 1784–1810. In red, blue, and gold. Incised on base of biscuit figures

DERBY 1795–96. Duesbury & Kean

DERBY. Copy of Meissen mark

BOW 1749–53. Incised

BOW 1749–53. Incised

BOW 1749–53. Incised

BOW 1758–75. In red. Possibly a Giles mark

BOW 1755–60. In underglaze blue

BOW 1758–75. On figures. Usually in blue

BOW 1758–75. In underglaze blue. Mostly on figures

LONGTON HALL 1750–58. In blue and incised underglaze

LOWDIN's (Lund's) Bristol c. 1750. Workman's mark

Bristoll 1750	LOWDIN's (Lund's) Bristol 1750
	WORCESTER 1751–60. Workman's mark. In red
	WORCESTER 1755–60. Pseudo-Chinese mark
	Chinese characters meaning "Great Ming" for comparison
	WORCESTER 1755–95. In red, blue, gold, and black
	WORCESTER 1757 onwards. On blue-printed wares
	WORCESTER 1755–83. In underglaze blue
	WORCESTER 1755–83. In underglaze blue
	WORCESTER. Pseudo-Meissen mark. Used from 1757
Flight	WORCESTER 1783–92. In blue
FLIGHTS	WORCESTER 1783–92. Impressed
Flight	WORCESTER 1789–92. In red and blue
B.F.B.	WORCESTER 1807–13. Impressed
Chamberlains Worc	WORCESTER 1800–20. Chamberlain's factory
C	CAUGHLEY. In underglaze blue
C	CAUGHLEY. In underglaze blue
S	CAUGHLEY. In underglaze blue
SALOPIAN	CAUGHLEY. Impressed
2	PLYMOUTH 1768–72. In blue, red, and gold
X	BRISTOL (Champion's factory). In blue enamel
x X	BRISTOL (Champion's factory). Pseudo-Meissen mark. In underglaze and enamel blue
B6	BRISTOL (Champion's factory). In blue enamel

Z B   ZACHARIAH BOREMAN. On a Derby mug c. 1780

S   JOHN DONALDSON. On a Worcester vase c. 1765–70

✳   ISAAC FARNSWORTH, repairer. On Derby *biscuit* figures and groups

△   JOSEPH HILL, repairer. On Derby *biscuit* figures and groups

oneual   JEFFREY O'NEALE. In a disguised form as part of an inscription. Chelsea
c. 1754

T°   TEBO 1749–80(?). The mark of a migratory repairer who worked at a number of factories. Impressed into body

WEDGWOOD

WEDGWOOD
WEDGWOOD

Mark upon Queen's Ware from 1769 until the present, and upon ornamental jasper, black basalt and terra cotta, from 1780 until the present. Recently the words Etruria and Barlaston and the name of the pattern have often been added.

Mark found inside the plinth of old basalt vases and sometimes on the pedestal of a bust or large figure.

Mark placed round the screw of basalt, granite and Etruscan vases.

WEDGWOOD
BONE CHINA
MADE IN
ENGLAND

Mark upon fine bone china from 1878 until the present, printed in sepia and other colours.

OF ETRURIA
WEDGWOOD
MADE IN
& ENGLAND
BARLASTON

Mark upon Queen's Ware from 1940 to the present, with the name of the pattern often added.

All photographs are by Hans Hinz, Basel with the exception of Plates 166 and 167 which are by Mrs. Anna Wachsmann, New York.

Printed by Hertig + Co. AG, Bienne. – Reproductions in four color offset lithography by Imprimeries Réunies S. A., Lausanne. – Reproductions for black and white illustrations by Atesa-Argraf, Geneva. – Binding by Mayer & Soutter S. A., Lausanne.

Printed in Switzerland

DATE DUE

DEMCO 38-297